FRENCH PLANNING

BY VERA LUTZ

AMERICAN ENTERPRISE INSTITUTE FOR PUBLIC POLICY RESEARCH

FRENCH PLANNING

By

Vera Lutz

May 1965

PUBLISHED AND DISTRIBUTED BY THE

AMERICAN ENTERPRISE INSTITUTE
FOR PUBLIC POLICY RESEARCH
WASHINGTON, D.C. 20036

Vera Lutz, who received her training in economics at the London School of Economics, is the author of several books and of numerous articles on economic affairs. Her latest book, "Italy: A Study in Economic Development" was published in 1962. The present study forms part of a larger study which she is making of French-style economic planning.

AMERICAN ENTERPRISE INSTITUTE
For Public Policy Research

THE AMERICAN ENTERPRISE INSTITUTE FOR PUBLIC POLICY RESEARCH, tablished in 1943, is a nonpartisan research and educational organization nich studies national policy problems.

Institute publications take two major forms:

1. LEGISLATIVE AND SPECIAL ANALYSES—factual analyses of current legislative proposals and other public policy issues before the Congress prepared with the help of recognized experts in the academic world and in the fields of law and government. A typical analysis features: (1) pertinent background, (2) a digest of significant elements, and (3) a discussion, pro and con, of the issues. The reports reflect no policy position in favor of or against specific proposals.

2. LONG-RANGE STUDIES—basic studies of major national problems of significance for public policy. The Institute, with the counsel of its Advisory Board, utilizes the services of competent scholars, but the opinions expressed are those of the authors and represent no policy position on the part of the Institute.

ADVISORY BOARD

CONTENTS

PREFACE

There are essentially two reasons for the popularity which "French-style" economic planning has achieved in a number of Western countries in recent years. One is the belief that it is a way of quickening the pace of economic growth. The other is its "softness" compared with "Eastern-style" planning.

In this study I have argued, first, that we cannot be sure that the total effect of French planning methods has been to help rather than hinder growth in France itself; secondly, that French-style planning is something without a definite shape or form. Hence we cannot rely on its "softness" being enduring or, alternatively, on permanence for its claim to be called "central planning of the economy."

This characteristic of being uneasily poised between two stools is what one French economist, Professor Daniel Villey, has called the "inherent instability of French planning." It was clearly discernable in 1964, when many Frenchmen of different shades of economic and political opinion were demanding a reversal of the government's policy of "abandoning the Plan in favor of market mechanisms" or of "reducing it to mere forecasting." "French-style" planning means very different things to different people in France today.

At the same time the ambition of those most directly concerned with the drawing up of the Plan is to embrace more and more aspects of economic development in their system of precisely figured targets and predictions. But the more complex and detailed the Plan becomes on paper, the greater is the danger of an exposed bluff unless the Plan is effectively implemented.

*　*　*

Shortly after the present study was completed, the government submitted the "Report on the Principal Options of the 5th Plan" (which will run from 1966 to 1970) first to the Economic and Social Council, and then to Parliament. This time the authorities are in one respect "playing safe." They proposed to "choose" a growth rate on the modest, instead of—as previously—the high side. The rate recommended is 5.0 percent, compared with the 4th Plan's 5.5 percent, which is now seen to have been overambitious, and incompatible with the maintenance of monetary stability. We may remark, however, that the claim that the public authorities have it in their power to "choose" the growth rate for their country's economy is not being dropped. This pretention was criticized, during the discussion of the "Report on the Options" in the Economic and Social Council, by Mr. Jacques Rueff, who warned against the danger of making exact prophecies. The Pythia of Delphi, prophetess of the Greek god Apollo, had, he said, been carefully trained "never to fix a date, and never to give any figures."

The 5th Plan is, however, to contain two innovations which go still further than the preceding Plans in the direction of quantifying policy aims. First, the programming in physical quantities, with which French planning was exclusively concerned in the past, is now to be accompanied by "programming in values" that is, by the rudiments of an "incomes policy." This will state, for example, the amount by which the retained earnings (self-finance) of firms should grow over the period of the Plan; the percentage by which annual earnings per head of the industrial labor force should increase; the (higher) percentage by which individual farm incomes should rise, and the percentage by which social security benefits should increase. The second innovation is a first step towards the quantification of regional development targets. It is declared to be "desirable and possible" to locate 35-40 percent of newly created industrial jobs in the "underdeveloped" western half of the country, which has at present about 37 percent of the population but only 24 percent of the industrial employment.

The presentation to Parliament of the "principal options" of the 5th Plan before its preparation enters the Commission stage is itself a new feature, aimed at the "democratization" of the Plan. After the big build-up which had been given to this new feature in anticipation, the actual event proved to be an anti-climax. The general expectation had been that a choice would be offered between a number of different "models" of economic development, each worked out in considerable detail. In fact only one of three variants (that connected with the 5.0 percent growth rate) was elaborated in detail, the two others (based on one lower and one higher growth rate, respectively) being presented only in very general terms. The planners seem in this instance to have recoiled before the immensities of their task.

A greater novelty, perhaps, in the matter of "options" was the presentation of a "counter-plan" drawn up by one of the Left-Wing political parties (the Unified Socialist Party). This was a Plan which, besides being based on a higher growth rate (5.5 percent) than that proposed by the government, demanded much more public intervention in the economy than was compatible with the "conservative neo-capitalist" line, as the authors of the counter-plan called it, of the present government. In the circumstances, the presentation of this "option" was of no more than formal significance. But it was another sign of the increasingly sharp divisions of opinion between planning schools to which I refer in the text of this study.

At the moment there exists a large measure of government intervention in the French economy, especially in the form of controls over prices and over issues of fixed-interest securities on the capital market. But this is connected not so much with "the Plan" as with the "stabilization plan" introduced in September 1963. Originally expected to be a necessity of six months' duration, this new struggle against inflation still continues after 15. It is not, therefore, certain at present whether the 5th Plan will start in conditions of re-established monetary stability, or in conditions similar to those in which the 3rd Plan was launched. Up till now, France's "stabilization plans," though almost as frequent as "the Plans," have been something separate and apart from the latter. This is another aspect of French planning which it is proposed to alter under the 5th Plan.

December 1964   VERA LUTZ

I.

INTRODUCTORY

In the early 1950's one of the most popular topics of current economic discourse was the "miracle" of the rapid postwar economic recovery of Western Germany, achieved by the policy of reverting to a market economy, freed from price controls, rationing, and priority allocations, a policy which Germany had not known for almost 20 years.

At the beginning of the 1960's a new source of wonder was drawing the attention of economists and economic policymakers. This was the rapid and regular economic growth achieved over the past decade by France. This was now attributed in good part to economic planning, of a special kind—invented in France — which might recommend itself to Western democracies by its

1

freedom from the elements of political authoritarianism and economic regimentation that were associated with planning of the Soviet type, or of the sort practiced in National Socialist Germany.

France's planning experience dates from 1947. The first, or "reconstruction" Plan, was sponsored by the post-Liberation Provisional Government, headed by General de Gaulle, and was drawn up, in 1946, under the supervision of Jean Monnet. Though originally intended to cover only the four years 1947-50, this Plan was later extended to 1952-53 in connection with the European Recovery Program of the United States, where it was welcomed in official circles as a way of assuring that France's share of Marshall Aid would be used for the approved purposes. The 2nd Plan covered the years 1954-57, the 3rd the years 1958-61, and the current Plan—the 4th—runs from 1962 through 1965. The 5th, to run from 1966 through 1970, is in preparation.

The Monnet Plan attracted a good deal of interest abroad, partly because of its tie-up with Marshall Aid, and partly because of its strong contrast to the methods adopted by certain other European countries for achieving the same ultimate ends. In the period following the Monnet Plan, however, foreign interest in French planning subsided. In the 1950's the aspect of French economic performance which drew most comment abroad was not the high average rate of growth of the national product, but the successive waves of inflation, leading to balance-of-payments difficulties, and culminating in the crisis of mid-1958, when the nation's gold and foreign exchange reserves had for the second time within six months virtually disappeared despite repeated recourse to foreign credits.

This situation necessitated the drastic program of financial rehabilitation undertaken in late 1958, of which one feature was a new devaluation of the franc (the second [1] since the general European currency alignment of September 1949, and the sixth since the liberation of France in 1944). The stabilization measures were based on recommendations of an

---

[1] The two devaluations, one in the summer of 1957 and the other at the end of 1958, together amounted to 30 percent.

official committee of which the chairman was Mr. Jacques Rueff, a liberal [2] economist no less strong in his convictions than Dr. Ludwig Erhard of Germany, and were carried out by a liberal Finance Minister, Mr. Antoine Pinay. They were the first big economic policy event after the return to power (in May 1958) of General de Gaulle and the setting up of the Fifth Republic. Though immensely important for the development of the French economy in the following years, they constituted, it should be noticed, an operation that was completely separate and distinct from the 3rd Plan which was supposed to be in force at the time.

Even in France the 2nd and 3rd Plans attracted comparatively little attention. The government did little to bring them before the public eye, and references to them in the press were rare. It was not until the 4th Plan was being prepared that interest began to increase. "The Plan" now became the subject of almost daily references in the press; began to be treated as one of the major themes of national economic and political life;

and struck a large part of French intellectual opinion with the force of a new religion. One of the reasons for this change was doubtless the public blessing given to the 4th Plan by General de Gaulle, and the corresponding seriousness with which it was taken by members of his government. In a speech delivered in May 1961, the General exhorted his countrymen to regard the achievement of the aims of the 4th Plan as an "ardent obligation" and to make the Plan *la grande affaire de la France.*

It was about this time, too, that French planning began to make a strong appeal to foreign economists and foreign governments. For instance, it was in the autumn of 1960 that the first feelers were being put out towards the adoption of something similar to French planning in Great Britain, leading to the establishment in the following year of the National Economic Development Council. This rather sudden "discovery" in Britain and elsewhere of French planning was probably not unconnected with the new state of general economic health which France was then en-

---

[2] The word "liberal" is here used in the European sense, i.e., as referring to protagonists of free enterprise and a market economy.

joying, as a result of the Pinay-Rueff reforms of 1958-59, and of the fact that for some time following these the rate of inflation of the French cost and price level was lower relatively to that in other countries than it had been previously. In 1959 and the next two years or so, France's products were clearly more competitive on world markets than they had been for a long time. Her balance-of-payments difficulties had ceased. And in 1960 the rate of growth of her gross national product was again high after the post-stabilization slowing of 1958-59.

The Pinay-Rueff stabilization measures could not by any stretch of the imagination be considered a part of French planning. Because of them the 3rd Plan had, in fact, been laid aside and replaced by an Interim Plan improvised for the occasion. Their consequences had, however, made France's economic performance look much better by 1960-61 than in earlier years, when the average rate of growth had been just as high but accompanied by financial instability. Foreign observers now began to take much closer notice of the fact that France's growth rate had been re-

markably high and comparatively regular throughout the 1950's. And many of them drew the conclusion that French planning must have something to do with this. This association of cause and effect came, not very surprisingly perhaps, chiefly from countries which had recently had lower growth rates than France, such as Britain, the United States, and Belgium, rather than from those which had achieved equally high or higher rates—without the benefit of French planning—such as West Germany, the Netherlands, or Switzerland. The OECD, in its Report on France published in the summer of 1962, joined in this chorus of praise for French planning, which had had the effect, it said, of making the efficiency of investments high.

One of the chief pieces of evidence in this connection is the following table, based on the annual rates of real growth in the gross national product in various countries as calculated by the OECD. These are shown in the table below. They are, of course, subject to the usual reservations concerning exactitude and comparability.

Gross National Product at Constant Prices:[1] Percentage Increase or Decrease (—) With Respect to Previous Years

	France[2]	U.S.A.	U.K.	Germany[3]	Italy	Belgium	Netherlands
1951	6.0	7.3	2.1	10.5	7.6	—	3.0
1952	2.5	3.7	—0.7	8.3	2.9	—	2.0
1953	3.1	4.1	4.3	7.5	7.6	—	8.5
1954	4.8	—1.6	4.3	7.4	5.1	3.7	7.3
1955	5.8	8.0	2.8	11.5	6.7	5.5	7.7
1956	5.0	1.9	2.7	6.9	4.2	2.5	3.9
1957	6.0	2.1	1.7	5.4	6.3	2.7	2.6
1958	2.5	—1.6	1.2	3.3	4.4	—1.0	0.5
1959	2.9	6.6	3.4	6.7	7.7	1.8	5.3
1960	7.5[4]	2.6	4.3	8.8	7.1	5.4	8.6
1961	4.5[4]	1.9	3.0	5.5	8.0	3.2	2.7
Average[5] 1950-61	4.6	3.1	2.6	7.4	6.1	2.9[6]	4.7
Coefficient of variation	0.35	0.97	0.55	0.30	0.27	—	0.58
1962	7.0	6.3	0.8	4.1	6.3	4.3	2.6
1963	4.3	3.3	3.7	3.2	4.8	3.6	3.6

[1] 1954 prices up to 1961; 1958 prices for 1962 and 1963. But see note 4.

[2] Gross product data incorporate revisions for years 1960 on which have not been extended to previous years. The new series has been linked to the old.

[3] Data for 1960 onwards include the Saar. In calculating the growth rates the development between 1960 and 1961 has been linked to the series for the previous years. Similarly for West Berlin, included from 1962 on.

[4] At 1959 prices.

[5] Geometric average annual percentage change.

[6] 1953-61 only.

We should add that France achieved her high average rate of growth with: (a) an almost stable employed labor force (at least up till 1961), contrasting sharply in this respect with Germany and Italy; and (b) an average ratio of gross fixed investment to gross national product perceptibly lower than that of Germany, Italy, or the Netherlands. Concerning the first point we may remark that between May 1954 and March 1962 (two successive Census of Population dates), while the total population of France increased by 8 percent, the size of the working population remained virtually unchanged, the proportion of the working population to the total falling from 45 percent to 41 percent. It was not until 1962, and the arrival of the "repatriates" from Algeria, that the working population began perceptibly to grow.

Statistical comparisons of the growth in gross national product per worker are even more difficult to make than those of the growth in gross national product itself, owing to the lack of accurate or comparable data on the size of the labor force. As near as we can tell, however, the product per worker grew between 1954 and 1962 by approximately the same proportion (some 46-47 percent) in France as in Germany.

It has been stressed that France's rate of economic growth, besides being high, has been more regular than that of other countries. In the table are shown the coefficients of variation [3] of the various countries' growth rates over the period of eleven years 1950-61. According to this measure of stability, France's record is, however, only about average. It is better than that of the United States, Britain, or the Netherlands, but not better than that of Germany or Italy.

The argument is that, because France has had high and regular growth along with her particular brand of economic planning, one thing must be due to the other. It suffers from the weakness of all *post hoc - propter hoc* arguments. Obviously numerous factors—other than French planning—in fact influenced postwar economic development in France both before and after 1958. It is not my task to examine all of these here. I shall concentrate on the one factor, French planning, in the attempt to see whether there are sufficient grounds for thinking that it justifies the confidence of its would-be imitators.

---

[3] S. Wickham, in "French Planning: Retrospect and Prospect," *Review of Economics and Statistics,* November 1963, p. 345, has calculated these coefficients for a few countries. Germany's coefficient is there shown as being somewhat too high, however, owing to the attribution to the growth rate of one of the years (1960) of the entire output of the Saar, which in that year was included in the figures of West Germany for the first time.

II.

THE NATURE OF FRENCH PLANNING

Why was it that the new kind of economic planning invented by the French had come by 1961-62 so to impress foreign observers. In seeking the answer we may recall a view of economic planning published in 1944, which attracted a great deal of contemporary attention particularly in the United States. It is that given by Professor F. A. Hayek in *The Road to Serfdom*.

The main thesis of this book was that economic planning meant traveling the road to totalitarianism. The definition of planning which Professor Hayek used on that occasion was "a central direction of all economic activity according to a single plan laying down how the resources of society would be 'consciously directed' to serve particular ends in a particular way."[1] He remarked further[2] that a distinction could, and should, be made between planning that was designed to bring about a more equal distribution of income, and planning conceived primarily as a method of running the economy, irrespective of the particular ends chosen, equal income distribution being only one of many possible ends. Although the centrally planned economy had once been widely alleged to be more efficient than the liberal or "unplanned" economy, this claim was, he thought, being progressively abandoned in Western countries. Many protagonists of planning now advocate it, he said, not "because of its superior productivity but because it will enable us to secure a more just and equitable distribution of wealth. This is indeed the only argument for planning which can be seriously pressed."[3]

Some 15 years later, a new phase had been reached in the changing fashions of thought about this subject. Some of the objectives of socialism had been achieved, in various Western countries, by other methods of State intervention than economic planning. The belief in the greater efficiency of a centrally planned economy, a belief that had for a while lost ground in some of these countries, was, thanks to the French example, once again very much to the fore. In "French" planning the emphasis had, in fact, so far been more on the efficiency aspect than on that of social justice. Many French Socialists denied that it was "real" planning. In Britain it was the Conservative party that was recommending the importation of French planning methods.

Although France can be said already to have had more than 15 years of continuous planning experience, we need to distinguish two phases, that of the first, or Monnet Plan, and that of the post-Monnet Plans. In the period immediately following the liberation, the discussions in France, concerning the way in which her economic recovery could be most quickly and efficaciously accomplished, had led to the adoption of the view that an active role must be played by the State. The next few years were consequently characterized by a policy

---

[1] Hayek, *op. cit.*, p. 35.
[2] *Ibid.*, pp. 32-34.
[3] *Ibid.*, pp. 98-99.

of economic *"dirigisme,"* as opposed to a quick return to a liberal, or market economy, which was the way that West Germany chose. This policy had three principal characteristics. First, it brought with it (in 1945-46) some important nationalizations, affecting the gas and electric power industries, almost the whole of coal mining, the Renault motor works, the Bank of France, the four large deposit banks, and the larger insurance companies. Secondly, it implied the retention for some years of most of the wartime system of price, rationing, and licensing controls. Thirdly, it gave the State, through the Monnet Plan, a dominant influence over the direction of investment.

This first Plan was essentially a plan for the reconstruction of the "basic" sectors of the economy: coal, electricity, steel, cement, transport, and agricultural equipment. Its primary objectives were set out in terms of the growth in capacity and output needed in these six sectors. The corresponding investments were, in large part, financed out of funds provided by the Treasury. This was true particularly of the nationalized industries, but also, though to a lesser extent, of the others. In the first three years of the Plan, for example, public funds provided for close to 60 percent, on the average, of France's gross fixed capital investments, though the proportion declined during the later years of the Plan. Controls over new capital issues and over the distribution of medium- and long-term credit, priority allocations of raw materials, building permits, and permits to install new equipment were other instruments for pushing investment and production into the chosen direction, that of "imposed reconstruction" as Mr. Pierre Massé, the present head of the planning Commissariat, once called it.[4] There was also the threat—which did not need to be carried out [5]—that firms would in case of need be commanded to produce certain goods.

By the beginning of the 1950's the worst scarcities had been overcome, and the bulk of the direct controls (rationing and allocations of goods, price and wage controls, etc.) had gradually been swept away. The control, partial or general, and for short or long periods,

---

[4] Pierre Massé, "Pratique et Philosophie de l'Investissement," *Economie Appliquée*, 1952.
[5] Pierre Bauchet, *La Planification française*, 1962, pp. 88-89.

over prices has remained a feature of French policy, as we shall see below. On the whole, however, French planning relied in the later years on less authoritarian methods than had been used in the early ones.

Referring to the difference between the first and the later Plans, commentators have said that the 2nd Plan was much more of a real "plan" than its predecessor, because it covered (as did the subsequent Plans) the whole of the economy, instead of only a limited number of sectors. In another sense, however, the Monnet Plan was the more "real." For the authorities had, especially in the early years of that Plan, a much firmer control over the direction of investment than they had under the later Plans. In any case, it is these post-Monnet Plans that have set the tone for what has come to be considered a special type of "French" planning, which is very different from Eastern, Soviet, planning, and different also from other forms of Western planning, such as Dutch.

The name given to this type of planning in France is *planification*

souple, which we may usually translate as "soft" planning, although it also carries the implication that the planning is "flexible" or, that is, adaptable, to changing events. It is distinguished from planning that is "coercive," in the sense of depending on the giving of orders to private economic operators by the public authorities. Professor Perroux [6] has described it as planning of "quasi-liberal inspiration." It is also called "indicative," as opposed to "imperative" planning. A favorite expression of Mr. Massé is "indicative but active" planning, by which is meant that French planning does not merely set out to forecast and describe the spontaneous development of the French economy—as the word "indicative" alone might lead us to suppose—but seeks to guide it towards the attainment of chosen objectives, and utilizes "instruments of execution" for so doing, instruments which consist, however, less in administrative orders and prohibitions than in the offering of incentives. It is also medium-term, as opposed to short-term (or annual) planning. These characteristics distinguish it not only

---

[6] François Perroux, *Le IVe Plan français,* 1962, p. 43.

from the economic policymaking of countries (e.g., West Germany) which do not pretend to have any sort of "central economic planning," but also from Dutch planning. The latter, although it has just as long a history as French planning, was in the past conducted on an annual basis only. It is, also, according to the general opinion in France, less conspicuously of an "active" character than French planning.

It is true that the first article of the law approving the 4th Plan describes it rather modestly as a "framework of investment programs for the period 1962-1965, and an instrument for orienting economic expansion and social progress." But Mr. Valéry Giscard d'Estaing, the Minister of Finance, remarked, in a context to which we shall refer later,[7] that it was not *merely* that. On the same occasion he said that "French planning seeks to be an acceptable compromise between freedom and obligation," and that part of the originality of the Plan is that the method of applying it is "equidistant from total liberalism and bureaucratic

planning." He was here expressing a view which had come to be shared by many people outside France, who thought they had found in French planning the perfect compromise: a system which gave the presumed benefits of central planning (better coordination of the activities of individual economic operators, and more conscious and more accurate prospecting of the future, and hence a more rational use of resources and higher productivity) but without sacrificing the fundamental liberties (political democracy, private property, freedom of enterprise, and freedom of consumers' choice).

In any discussion of comparative systems of "central economic planning," it must be kept in mind that this term has now come to be used in a much looser sense than would have been generally accepted 20 years ago. The term is, in fact, now often used to describe any well-coordinated, rational, and forward-looking official economic policy, especially if this is based on either short- or long-term forecasting of future economic developments. According to this usage, any govern-

---

[7] See pp. 32-33 below. The occasion was that of the Parliamentary debate on the 4th Plan in May 1962.

ment that is making efforts to render its general economic policy more coherent is engaging in "central economic planning" whether it chooses to call what it is doing by this name or not. The government of West Germany, for example, is said to be "allergic" to the word "planning." This modern definition is a far cry from that given by Hayek in 1944 and quoted above. It is a very much broader definition which covers up some important distinctions. Even if we are not "allergic" to the use of the term "central economic planning" to describe what might simply be called a "rational economic policy," there seems to be a case for introducing a new terminological distinction, and for saying that "central economic planning" in its new meaning is something different

from "central planning of the economy," the first *not necessarily* implying the second. French planning *has* aimed at better planning by the government within the latter's traditional sphere of activity, but it has also aimed at something more. In theory at least it is a system for centrally "guiding," "coordinating," or "directing" (by "soft" methods) the whole economy.

How far the practice has followed the theory is one of the questions we must try to answer. But the underlying conception is what may be called "central planning of the economy"; and generally speaking the meaning attached in France today to the term "economic planning" is closer to the old usage than the new.

III.

THE ADMINISTRATIVE MACHINERY AND THE PREPARATION OF THE PLAN

The Planning Authorities

The organizational and administrative machinery on which French planning relies, and the method of preparing the Plans have been described at considerable length elsewhere.[1] The brief account that follows is confined to some of the most important aspects.

The Planning Office or Commissariat au Plan reports to the Prime Minister. Its head, or Commissaire général does not have ministerial rank. The staff of his office is small: it recently numbered about 150 persons, inclusive of all grades down to the very lowest. A large contribution towards the work of

---

[1] Cf. Bauchet, *op. cit.*, and John and Anne-Marie Hackett, *Economic Planning in France*, 1963.

preparing the Plan comes, however, from other public or semi-public offices, and from private firms.

The planning machinery at present includes three supervisory and consultative bodies. One is an Interministerial Committee for the Plan, which consists of the Prime Minister, the Minister of Finance, and other Ministers responsible for the activities covered by the Plan.

The second is the Conseil supérieur du Plan, a body of some 60 members, presided over by the Prime Minister. The role of this Council has, however, been relatively unimportant. A proposal is under consideration for abolishing it since it overlaps with another body, representing the same interests, performing largely the same functions, and containing some of the same persons as members.

This third body is the Economic and Social Council (Conseil économique et social), which dates back to 1946, but had a much earlier predecessor in the National Economic Council established in 1925 and reformed in 1936. It has some 200 members who are appointed for terms of five years. About two-thirds of them are chosen by the groups they represent (the four trade union confederations, employers, farmers, "family associations," [2] artisans, etc.), and the other third are nominated directly by the government. For purposes of dealing with specialized problems the Council is divided into sections. One of these, the Investment and Planning Section, plays a particularly important role in connection with the preparation of the Plan.

The Council's function is to advise the government not merely on matters directly connected with the Plan, but on current economic and social problems in general. It normally meets once or twice a month, and its sessions usually last one or two days.

The Modernization Commissions

The so-called "Modernization Commissions," one of the inventions of Jean Monnet, constitute the part of the planning machinery which is generally regarded as most original. Especially outside France they are also one of the most con-

---

[2] These are organizations representing the interests of families, or, broadly speaking, consumers.

troversial aspects of the Plan. The members of these Commissions are nominated on the occasion of the preparation of each Plan by the Prime Minister on the recommendation of the Commissaire au Plan. The object of this method of selection and appointment is to ensure as far as possible that the members should participate in the discussions of the Plan as individuals with special knowledge of particular branches or problems rather than as spokesmen of pressure groups. Normally the Commissions do not také votes on the subjects discussed. The members are unpaid.

The number of Commissions has increased from Plan to Plan. For the 1st Plan there were 18; for the 4th Plan 27; and the 5th will have a few more. Most of the Commissions are what are called "vertical" Commisions, each dealing with an individual sector of activity. For the 4th Plan 22 vertical Commissions were constituted. The list of sectors was as follows: agriculture; fishing; food-processing; oil fuels; power; mines and nonferrous metals; steel; chemicals; manufacturing industries; artisan

activities; building and public works; transport; trade; housing; tourist industry; post and telecommunications; radio and television; cultural equipment; educational equipment; health and social equipment; urban equipment; overseas territories. Most sectors of the economy were thus covered. Still not represented were, however, numerous "tertiary" activities, as well as national defense. There were also five "horizontal" Commissions dealing respectively with: general economic and financial aspects; manpower; productivity; research; and regional planning.

The Commission members for the 4th Plan numbered nearly 1,000, and individual Commissions mostly had 30-50 members. The Commissions were, however, divided up into working parties containing many more people than the actual Commission members. In fact the total number of people directly participating in the Commission work in 1960-61 was over 3,000. They were divided as follows as regards the interests they represented:[3]

Farmers 107
Industrialists, artisans, and

---

[3] Cf. Bauchet, *op. cit.*, p. 48.

other heads of firms 715
Civil servants and other
officials 781
Representatives of trade un-
ions and peasants' organiza-
tions 281
Representatives of employers'
organizations 562
Others (experts) 691

A common criticism of this list concerns the smallness of the number of trade union representatives. The Commissions for the 5th Plan will contain a much larger number. There have also been complaints that the role of the trade unionists in the work of the Commissions has usually been a minor one. A generally admitted difficulty has, however, been that of finding enough union representatives with sufficient technical training for the kind of work involved.

How the Plan is Drawn Up

The way in which the Plan is prepared may be described by a very rapid sketch of the procedure adopted in the case of the 4th Plan.

The work of drafting the Plan was long. It took place in three main stages stretching over a period of nearly three years (1959-61). The first stage, lasting over a year,

consisted in the elaboration by the Commissariat, aided by the Economic and Financial Research Department of the Ministry of Finance and other official statistical and research offices, of a preliminary view of the prospects of economic development, by broad sectors of activity, over the years up to 1965 (but within a longer perspective extending up to 1975). These calculations were based on the hypothesis of three alternative rates of annual growth (3, 4.5, and 6 percent) in the economy as a whole.

At this stage, the figures were preliminary forecasts of "spontaneous tendencies" of economic development,[4] the main object being to discover the maximum growth rate that might be aimed at while maintaining internal and external financial equilibrium. The results obtained were submitted to the Investment and Planning Section of the Economic and Social Council, which *inter alia* expressed itself in favor of setting the growth rate on the high side (i.e., at 6 percent). Mr. Massé took the view that aiming so high would put too great a strain on the French economy, and wanted a rate of between 5.0

[4] *Ibid.*, p. 55.

and 5.5 percent. Other experts were still more cautious, regarding the rate of 5.5 (which was that ultimately chosen) as being beyond France's possibilities, and favoring the rate of 5.0.

Following these deliberations, the government instructed the Commissaire to adopt the growth rate of 5.0 percent as the basis for the Plan, but to give consideration also to the rate of 5.5. It informed him also of other general policy directives, and in particular of the desirability of this time increasing the volume of "social investments."

The second stage, which again took nearly a year (summer 1960 to spring 1961), was that at which the Commissions came into action. Taking the "indicative" framework given by the Commissariat's preliminary forecasts by broad sectors (or branches), each vertical Commission worked out the details for its branch, and in so doing checked the forecasts of the Commissariat. The limited number (28) of broad product and service groups dealt with by the Commissariat were now broken down into sub-groups.

What this meant concretely was that, for example, textiles, which figured as a single branch among the 28, was now divided into its various product sectors (wool, cotton, silk, etc.); that the chemicals branch was split up into some 60 products or product groups, and so on. Each Commission made, for the terminal year of the Plan, and for its branch, estimates that were finally set out in the form of three tables of questionnaire type. The first related to output, to the way in which this would be absorbed among the broad groups of uses regularly distinguished in the national income accounts (i.e., "intermediate" consumption, consumption by households, consumption by the administrations, investments in fixed capital, exports), and to the necessary volume of imports. The second table related to the necessary amounts of labor of different grades. The third referred to the investments required in various classes of fixed capital, and to the manner in which the total investment might be financed (how much out of retained earnings and how much with outside funds) .[5]

---

[5] The labor table for the 4th Plan contained an innovation with respect to the preceding plans. It included the question of how the total number of persons employed by the branch could be expected to be distributed among the 21 regions distinguished in France's "regional development program."

On all the tables the Commissions also had to fill in data, following the same scheme, concerning the actual situation in their branches as it was in each of a number of preceding years.

During this stage information was exchanged between the Commissions in order to obtain inter-branch harmony. In theory the Commissariat's preliminary forecasts for some of the larger aggregates might get corrected as a result of the detailed research work done by the Commissions. In practice, however, as Professor Bauchet remarks, the Commissions "have most often largely confirmed them." [6]

It seems fair to conclude from the various published accounts, and from the privately expressed views of people who have served on the Commissions, that the Plan, so far as its most significant figures (i.e., the broad aggregates, as opposed to the narrower sub-aggregates) are concerned, is essentially the work of the Commissariat and the services mentioned above, and that the role of the Modernization Commissions in this particular con-

nection is comparatively small, even if they serve other purposes which will be described below. This would mean that the key items in the medium-term forecasts really are made by the authorities, which thus assume a responsibility for the whole set of detailed forecasts based upon these items.

The data obtained from all the branches in accordance with the common scheme are finally added together and checked for overall consistency (or "coherence" in the language of the Commissariat), and here the horizontal Commissions play an important part. Where serious discrepancies appear the Commissariat sees that they are "corrected." [7] Great importance is attached by the planners to the fact that the Plan's final figures have passed this "consistency test." [8]

In the case of the 4th Plan, after a first rough synthesis had been made, early in 1961, on the basis of a growth rate of 5.0 percent, and had shown that this rate might easily be exceeded, the Commissions were requested to do the work all over again for a growth rate

---

[6] *Op. cit.,* p. 166.
[7] For further remarks on how this is done, see pp. 77-79 below.
[8] See pp. 77 ff.

half a point higher (5.5 percent), this being the rate that was eventually adopted. Most people agreed that this repetition of the procedure, which put an extremely heavy burden on the Commissions, should be avoided in the future.

The third stage was that of making the final synthesis, with the necessary last harmonizing adjustments and corrections. This was a joint effort of the Commissariat (again aided by the Economic and Financial Research Department of the Ministry of Finance), the Modernization Commissions, and several Ministries. When this work had been completed, and the Plan approved by the government, its broad outline was hurriedly submitted to the Conseil supérieur du Plan, in October 1961, and the whole draft was put before the Economic and Social Council in November. The Plan was finally presented in December to Parliament as an annex (a document of some 580 pages)[9] to a bill proposing its approval and containing a two-page summary of its contents. Its passage into law occurred late in July 1962, when half of the first year of the Plan was already

over. Even so, the whole timetable from start to finish had been very tight.

This was the first of the four Plans to be submitted to Parliament before it came into force. The 1st Plan had been ordered by a decree of January 1946. The text of the 2nd was presented to the National Assembly in plenary session nearly 18 months after it came into force, and became "law" two and a quarter years after (i.e., in March 1956). The 3rd Plan was promulgated by Presidential decree, one and a quarter years after it had started (i.e., in March 1959). This procedure has been widely criticized as being undemocratic.

The Contribution of Parliament

The 4th Plan, before being debated in plenary session by each of the two Houses of Parliament, had been examined by several of their Parliamentary Commissions. Certain changes were made during this process. They were largely connected with the necessities imposed by new problems that had arisen since the Plan was tabled.

In the National Assembly the debates in plenary session occupied

---

[9] This figure refers to the second of two editions of different format.

most of its time for a month, and in the Senate they filled the greater part of two weeks. As was officially recognized, however, Parliament had little possibility of effectively modifying the Plan's contents. Mr. Giscard d'Estaing, the Minister of Finance, remarked that amendments affecting the Plan's figures would deprive it of its character. The debate obviously had to be confined to general policy issues.

Some adjustments were made in the text of the Plan to give expression to Parliament's special concern with certain questions, such as the problems connected with the arrival of the "repatriates" from Algeria. And, most important, a clause was inserted obligating the government to a "democratization" of the procedure for the 5th Plan. The clause specified that the government should, before giving its directives to the Commissaire, submit to Parliament the "main options" involved. On the second and final reading of the bill in the National Assembly, the Socialists and Communists voted against adoption. In the view of these groups, "indicative" and "voluntary" planning was not the real thing, and

the Plan was insufficiently concerned with social objectives.

In the Assembly 110 deputies (out of some 480) had spoken on the Plan. Most of the deputies had apparently shown less interest than many partisans of the democratization of the Plan had expected. Two other extremely important debates had, however, competed for their attention during the period concerned. One was concerned with events in Algeria, and the other with foreign policy. There was the problem of pressure on the Parliamentarian's time, as well as of the difficulty of the highly technical subject matter. Last, but not least, there was the limitation on the scope of the debate to which the Minister of Finance had referred.

The contribution of Parliament to the Plan on this occasion had obviously been minimal. Nevertheless great importance was attached to this first step, and the promise of others, towards more "democratic" planning.

Cost of the Plan

The planners have sometimes remarked that the smallness of the Planning Commissariat's staff and of its annual budget (about

12 million NF [10] in 1962) is apt to give an overmodest impression of the importance of the Plan. It would seem quite expensive if allowance were made for all the time devoted to the Plan by the many outside collaborators including not only staff members of other government offices but also the people working in the Modernization Commissions, and all those, probably numbering a few tens of thousands, who do the research, paper, and copying work backstage, on their firms' time. This is not denied by the planners, who, however, judge the results to be worth the cost. It is nonetheless an exaggeration to describe the Plan, as some of its partisans have done, as a market research service offered "free" by the government to business.

---

[10] The New Franc, equivalent to 100 old francs, was introduced at the beginning of 1960. Its exchange value approximates 20.2 cents.

IV.

OBJECTIVES AND OPTIONS

The notion of "fundamental options," now considered so important in connection with the democratization of French planning, did not explicitly appear in any of the Plans prior to the 4th. Even this referred to only two essential options. One was that of a high growth rate in preference to a more modest one, which would have demanded less effort from the nation both in the form of work (permitting a reduction in working hours)[1] and in the form of saving or investment. The second option concerned the way in which the increased output should be used, the choice falling here on the

[1] In fact there did occur in 1963, a big extension of the practice of according to workers a fourth week of paid holidays.

23

allocation of a larger part than in the previous Plans to "social investments" (in public education, in municipal equipment, in hospitals, in the water supply system, in the advancement of research, etc.) . To mark this change in emphasis the Plan was given the title "Plan for Social and Economic Development," instead of "Modernization and Equipment Plan" which was that borne by each of the first three Plans.

In the law approving the 4th Plan a clause was inserted stipulating that Parliament should decide upon the principal options when the next Plan was prepared. It mentioned the following five subjects: the expansion of the economy; the distribution of gross domestic production between investment and consumption; the desirable structure of final consumption; the direction to be followed by social policy; and the direction to be taken by regional policy. Obviously these five subjects alone were, even if only two or three choices were presented under each, capable of giving rise (through the many permutations between them) to a great many "variants" between which Parliament would have to choose.

The "fundamental objectives" of the Plan have since the 2nd Plan been fairly similar from Plan to Plan. Here I shall concentrate on those of the 4th Plan. They may be listed under five heads.

The first aim was an increase in gross domestic output of 24 percent in the four years, implying an average annual growth rate (compound) of 5.5 percent. (This was higher than the rates, of 4.6 and 4.9 respectively, aimed at in the 2nd and 3rd Plans.)

The second aim was to ensure full employment of the labor force, which was going to grow faster over the next four years than previously, the increase being estimated at 660,000 persons (including "repatriates" and immigrants).

The third aim was to attain a high level of foreign trade, and to achieve a small surplus in the balance of payments after provision for debt repayment and aid to underdeveloped areas, and hence to strengthen the country's foreign exchange reserves.

The fourth aim was to give priority regarding income expansion to the least favored classes and regions, and in particular to promote the "tendency towards income parity" for the farming population in relation to other economic groups,[2] and to encourage balanced regional development.

The Plan did not do much towards quantifying this fourth aim. The 3rd Plan had set precise target prices (in francs of constant purchasing power) for 1961, to be approached in annual stages, for seven of the most important agricultural products, though the system was twice modified, first in January 1959 (in connection with the measures taken to deal with the financial crisis of 1958), and then in November 1960, after which it in effect came to an end. The procedure of fixing prices four years in advance, which had been severely criticized for its rigidity, was not re-adopted in the 4th Plan. One reason was the new regulations which were about to be established for the European Common Market, leaving France a less independent hand in the fixing of her domestic farm prices.

Regarding the regional distribution of economic development, the Plan gives figures only for the estimated spontaneous increase in the demand for and supply of manpower in nonagricultural activities, for the consequent surpluses or deficits in the individual regions, and hence for the extent of the interregional labor migration that would have to take place if "spontaneous employment tendencies" [3] had their way. The arresting of industrial concentration in the Paris region, and the attenuation of the regional disparities in economic development, have been a constant aim of government policy since 1955. The aim had already found its place in the 3rd Plan, but neither this nor the 4th Plan attempted to set out "objectives" or "forecasts" for regional investment and production, or to map a regional distribution pattern for new industrial development.

The fifth aim was to raise the level of gross fixed investment to 22 percent of disposable resources (gross domestic output plus imports minus exports) in the Plan's

---

[2] It is roughly estimated that individual farmers' incomes on the average—though there are big differences from farm to farm—are only 50-60 percent of the average earnings level in the nonagricultural sector. The government's aim of removing the relative income-inferiority of the agricultural population is coupled with a second aim, difficult to reconcile with the first, of enabling a large number of small family farms, many of them on poor land, to survive against the forces that would, in the absence of government intervention, lead to their absorption into larger units, or abandonment.

[3] Cf. Text of the 4th Plan, pp. 120 ff.

terminal year (the figure in 1961 having been only 20 percent).[4] This implied an increase in gross investment of 30 percent over the four years. In a sense this aim is subordinate to others. It is linked with the aims of raising social investments by 50 percent, while providing for the rise (28 percent) in "productive" investments necessary to achieve the target growth rate, and for an increase of 25 percent in investment in housing. The big increase in social investments was especially emphasized as a distinguishing mark of the 4th Plan compared with its predecessors.

The Plan anticipated that the increase in private consumption compatible with the other elements of the Plan would be 23 percent (equivalent to 5.3 percent per year), or 20 percent per head of the population, account being taken of the estimated increase in the latter.

A matter about which very little has been said in the Plans is changes in the structure of relative prices. While the planning authorities naturally recognize that future changes in relative incomes, costs and prices are bound to affect the consumption pattern of the future, these changes are a matter about which the Plans—inevitably perhaps—have found it difficult to make detailed forecasts.[5] Only two special cases, the prices of agricultural products and rents, have been explicitly mentioned by the Plans in this connection. The 3rd Plan, with its system of target prices for the seven agricultural products, had aimed at altering the relative price structure in order to increase the output of products in scarce supply and to limit the output of those of which there were surpluses. The 4th Plan again spoke of the general necessity of raising some agricultural prices compared with others,[6] and in particular

---

[4] This ratio is, for several reasons, higher than the ratio of gross fixed investment to gross national product, the ratio on which the international comparisons are generally based.

[5] Some attempt was made to deal with this problem in the preparation of the 4th Plan. The preliminary forecasts made by the Commissariat and passed to the Commissions were based on the working hypothesis of stable relative prices as well as a stable general price level. The Commissions were, however, asked to indicate such changes as they expected in the prices of the products of their branches relative to the general price level, so that, where the deviations were important, errors due to the preliminary assumption of constant relative prices might be corrected.

[6] Cf. Text of the 4th Plan, pp. 294-95.

promised a rise (absolute as well as relative) in the price of beef. It also referred to the need for bringing controlled rents on old housing to normal levels.[7]

In speaking of the general price level, all the Plans since the 2nd have been explicitly anti-inflationary in tone. The 2nd Plan [8] said that its preparation had been "dominated by the major preoccupation of realizing economic expansion within monetary stability." The 3rd Plan spoke of the re-establishment of monetary stability (after the inflation of 1956-57) as one of the conditions for the achievement of its aims. The Interim Plan also envisaged "approximate stability of the general price level." The 4th Plan referred to the damage done to the French economy in the past by inflation, and to the necessity of "maintaining monetary stability," of avoiding "excessive" rises in prices and wages, and of seeing that French prices do not rise relatively to those of other countries.[9]

None of the Plans contained targets or forecasts regarding the structure of incomes, or what might be called an "incomes policy." The failure to provide for such a policy had, by the time the 4th Plan got under way, come to be regarded by French planners as a major weakness.

Looking at the fundamental objectives of the Plan, we may notice that, with one important exception, they have had quite similar counterparts in the economic programs of other governments which have not so far adopted "French planning," or even any planning at all. The exception is the commitment, four years in advance, to a precise growth rate, and, through this, to a precise investment rate.

The Sub-Aggregates

The 4th Plan saw the increase in aggregate domestic output (of 24 percent) as being distributed over nine broad sectors of the economy as follows (the figures are again percentage increases between 1961 and 1965):

Agriculture	19
Fuel and power	24
Metal production	23
Chemicals	29
Manufacturing industries	23

---

[7] *Ibid.*, p. 26.
[8] Cf. Text of the 2nd Plan, p. 10.
[9] Cf. Text of 4th Plan, pp. 1, 21, 92, 103.

Building and building
  materials 32
Transport and
  communications 21
Housing (service) 23
Other services 27

These nine sectors were further
subdivided into individual products and services, or groups of
such products and services. Not all
of these details are to be found in
the document called "The 4th
Plan." For some of them we have
to go to the Reports of the Commissions, or to the Reports on the
Execution of the Plan.

In referring to the more detailed
analysis, even for the nine big sub-
aggregates listed above, the Plan
often speaks of "forecasts" (*pré-
visions*) rather than of "targets"
(*objectifs*). It is doubtless characteristic of planning which is "indicative but not merely so" that
there can be no very precise distinction between these two things. The
2nd Plan had distinguished the
"overall objectives" (or targets)
from the sectoral targets, but had
used the term "target" for all sectors and sub-sectors indiscrimin-
ately. This usage was probably a
carryover from the Monnet Plan
which, for the six basic sectors,
was quite definitely concerned with

targets. The 3rd Plan was the first
to suggest that the concept of the
"target" should be applied to only
some of the Plan's figures, and not
to others. In describing the results
of the 2nd Plan, it drew a distinction, retroactively so to speak, between the "basic" activities (power,
steel, and cement) for which "precise programs" or "targets" had
been set, and manufacturing industries, for which it was a question
"less of fixing imperative targets
than of establishing forecasts fitting into the framework of the
overall expansion targets."

Nonetheless, the 3rd Plan, with
reference to its own figures, sometimes used the two terms inter-
changeably, and at other times
consistently used one or the other,
but without making it clear
whether any real difference was
meant. The 4th Plan again remarked that "a distinction has to
be made between the basic products and services and the almost
infinite assortment of manufac-
tured goods. In the first case, the
programs must be kept on pain of
risking failure to realize the growth
target. In the second case, a certain
flexibility is both possible and desirable, substitutions between products taking place according to the

evolution of relative prices and of consumers' preferences." [10]

All the same the line between what are essential objectives or targets and what are forecasts only, and again between these and mere conjectures is not, and probably cannot—under "indicative" or "soft" planning—be a very clear one. This fact has inevitably given rise to doubts and misunderstandings as to the meaning of the Plan.

One instance where the 4th Plan made a quite precise distinction, but for a very special reason, between forecasts and targets was in connection with the problem of the growing surpluses of certain agricultural products. This is a problem which the government's policy of support prices and other forms of intervention, after 1953, had on the whole aggravated rather than mitigated. This was despite the fact that certain adjustments had been made in the relative price structure for the various products.

The 4th Plan referred, in much the same terms as its predecessors had done, to the necessity of orient-ing production towards the commodities for which the domestic demand was increasing rapidly, and for which the export possibilities were also good, (e.g., beef, fruit, and vegetables, other than potatoes) rather than towards those of which domestic consumption was stable or only increasing slowly, and for which the export outlets were also unremunerative (such as cereals and milk). But the Plan took it for granted that the quantities produced in 1965 of several important products—soft wheat, barley, maize, and milk—would exceed, and in some cases greatly exceed, the quantities that ought to be aimed at, and for which the government could expect to be able to guarantee a market, even in view of the new priorities which France would in the future enjoy on the markets of her partners in the European Economic Community. For each of these surplus products the Plan contrasted the forecast, or probable output with the target, or "desirable" output.

---

[10] *Ibid.*, p. 36.

V.

HOW THE PLAN WORKS

As already mentioned, one of the advantages claimed for the Plan is that it leads to better coordination of official economic policy. It[1] provides a natural meetingplace, the planners say, for the Ministers concerned with the various branches of economic affairs. Many planners think that this purpose would be still better served if the Commissaire au Plan were expressly vested with the function of overall coordination. They point out that the various Ministers in charge of departments dealing with economic matters have up to now remained free to act independently of him, and in this way, they say, part of the potential benefit of the Plan has been lost. Some of them

---

[1] I follow the French habit of sometimes using the expression "The Plan" in a personalized sense similar to that attached to "The Treasury," "The Fund," etc., in Anglo-Saxon countries.

propose the creation of a Ministry of the Plan whose head would be responsible for the Plan and for interministerial coordination; and others would go as far as to set up a superministry for Economic Affairs and the Plan, to which the Ministry of Finance as well as other government departments would be subordinate.

Judging by outward appearances at least, it seems evident that the Commissaire, though he does not have ministerial rank, and still less one that places him above other Ministers, has come especially in the last few years, to exert a substantial influence over economic policy. This is so even if the job of ultimate coordinator falls more largely, and naturally in some people's view, to the Minister of Finance. In part, of course, the extent of the Commissaire's influence has depended on the attitude assumed by the Minister of Finance towards the Plan, on the strength of his sense of commitment to it, and on the amount of attention he draws to it in public. We should remember also the boost given to the Plan in the spring of 1961 by the Head of the State.

The present Finance Minister, Mr. Giscard d'Estaing, who took office in January 1962, described himself, when speaking in the debate on the 4th Plan in the National Assembly in May that year, as taking the Plan more seriously than Mr. Paul Ramadier, a predecessor, had on a similar occasion, taken the 2nd Plan. He recalled Mr. Ramadier's statement in 1956 that the government was not "bound to a rigorous execution of the Plan," and contrasted this with his own action in recently directing his colleagues to subordinate the budget for the coming year (1963) to the pursuit of the objectives fixed by the 4th Plan. A few weeks later, before the Senate, the Minister made an even stronger promise of his allegiance. "For the first time," he said, "the Minister of Finance was making the aims of the Plan his own" and the latter was no longer "in the eyes of the State a mere framework of orientation." [2] In fact, as we shall have further occasion to remark, the definition of what is meant by "rigorously executing the Plan" is one of the most obscure aspects of French planning; and it may have

---

[2] This was the description of the Plan given in the text of the latter. See pp. 10-11 above.

been as much a mystery to Mr. Ramadier in 1956 as it still was to many an outsider, Frenchman or foreigner, in 1964. In any case, Mr. d'Estaing's avowed enthusiasm for the Plan failed to save it from virtual abandonment when (in 1963-64) he found himself obliged to give priority to his program for arresting inflation.

The existence of the Plan does not, of course, guarantee that French policy as a whole is necessarily more free from internal contradictions than the policy of many another country which does not have French planning. Some of the planners themselves complain of the still very imperfect coordination, which they propose to remedy in one of the ways mentioned above. These proposals remain a controversial matter, however, and it seems unlikely that, in the near future at any rate, the Minister of Finance will be deprived of his supremacy.

A second advantage claimed for the Plan is that it creates a "better-informed" economy, leading to a reduction of uncertainty, and to better coordination of the activities of the economic operators as well as to the better coordination of government policy already mentioned.

The forecasting done by the Commissariat, the statistical and other research work done by the Modernization Commissions, the publicizing of the forecasts (which might in the absence of the Plan have remained business secrets) made by individual industries, and the reports on their respective branches which the Commissions write up (besides filling in the questionnaire)—all these belong to this informing process. And so do the "dialogues"— a much used word in France today—which take place within the Commissions between government officials and industrialists, between firm and firm, occasionally at least between trade union official and employer, and so on.

The dialogues in the Commissions have been interpreted by some foreign observers, at least, as a euphemism for two kinds of activity which they regard with suspicion. The first is the reaching of understandings between firms for engaging in "restrictive practices." This does not, it should be noted, mean that the Plan officially does anything such as sharing out investment or production quotas among firms. The "planning" is not at present done at the level of the firm, but only at the level of the branch or sub-branch. What is meant is that the Commission meetings provide the occasion for firms to engage in collusion by themselves, perhaps with a certain amount of encouragement from the authorities. Frequently quoted in this connection is Adam Smith's dictum that "People of the same trade seldom meet together . . . but the conversation ends in a conspiracy against the public, or in some contrivance to raise prices." The second suspect activity is bargaining by entrepreneurs for favors (subsidies, tax relief, privileged finance, price increases) from the authorities as a condition for realizing the objectives set by the Plan. Such "favors" belong to the recognized instruments for implementing the Plan, and will be treated in more detail below. In short the Modernization Commissions are regarded by some people as the most useful part of the planning machinery, and by others as the most dangerous.

Commentators in the United States and West Germany have held them to be incompatible with those countries' antitrust or anti-cartel legislation. It is a question,

however, whether the industrialists concerned would not have almost as good an opportunity for making such arrangements through other channels if the Commissions did not exist. It is a question also whether in oligopolistic situations, in which only a limited number of firms can produce the same or a similar product if they are to reach optimum or near-optimum size, certain agreements, formal or informal, as to the division of activities between them, and the centralization of research work which they need in common, are not inevitable as a means of avoiding economic waste. In France, in any event, the official view is that the situation there is at present not comparable to that of the two countries mentioned; and fears are of a different order. The official attitude in the postwar period has been explicitly to encourage regroupings (including mergers) leading towards greater concentration and specialization of production, as a reaction against the excessive dispersion which characterized the French economy in the past.

Such regroupings are among the activities for which special incentives have been offered by the Plan.

The Law of August 1953 concerning inter-firm agreements, and the Commission which is responsible for investigating infringements of that law, seek to distinguish between "bad" agreements (providing for production quotas or other practices aimed at keeping prices high, such as retail price maintenance, refusal to sell, and so on) and "good" agreements (which lead, for example, to an increase in productivity). And mergers are often welcomed with the same considerations in mind. At present what is emphasized in France is that so much of her industry is still operating on too small a scale compared with the situation in other advanced industrial countries. It is generally conceded that a certain number of desirable regroupings have, in fact, taken place as a result of the procedure of "consultation and persuasion" in the Commissions. Many students of the subject abroad (e.g., in Britain, which is regarded as having a similar problem) judge this to be a highly commendable aspect of the French planning machinery, even if some of them would reject much else in French planning as useless or even harmful.

No doubt the meetings of the Commissions have also in many instances performed a useful educational function, for example, by encouraging the adoption of more rational methods of evaluating market prospects, of determining the profitability of investments, and of making other calculations helpful to successful business decisions. This is said to be especially true of some of the smaller firms, and of some whole sectors where the small and medium-sized firm dominates. The research work done by, or for the account of, the Commissions has led to notable improvements also in the quantity and quality of the available statistical material, though the biggest contribution from this side was probably made in the early years. The Commission meetings have also provided a forum—not the only one of course, but perhaps a particularly convenient one—where businessmen may draw the attention of government officials to genuine grievances regarding government policy and regulations, and where the officials may help to clarify the government's intentions.

This "informing function" of the Commissions is, however, surely dissociable (if we except one aspect which I shall discuss later [3] and' which is of doubtful effectiveness) from the vast amount of figuring which goes into the forecasting of precise future growth rates. If it were to be considered the Commissions' main task, it could presumably be accomplished more economically under some other terms of reference. And, by itself, it could not properly be called "central planning of the economy."

Achieving better coordination of economic policy and making the economy in general better-informed, are indeed not the only ways in which "French planning" is supposed to influence the course of economic events. The planners emphasize that the Plan not only has definite objectives, such as have been described above, but also "instruments of execution." It is these which make it something more than "indicative"; they make it also "active," and therefore a "Plan in the real sense," as opposed to a mere set of forecasts of the way in which the economy is likely to move spontaneously. Professor Bauchet remarks,[4] "planning that was only 'indicative,' or that is to say in which the State was concerned only with foreseeing the future and not with transforming it and organizing it, would not deserve the name."

---

[3] See pp. 77 ff below.
[4] *Op. cit.*, p. 33.

VI.

THE INSTRUMENTS

Price and Other
Administrative Controls

All the descriptions of the instruments mention price controls as belonging to them. As in many other countries, so also in France, the sector of the economy most affected by price-fixing has been agriculture. In private industry price controls were as a general rule gradually relaxed after 1948. In certain basic industries, e.g., steel and aluminum, they were, however, retained, increases in prices always requiring the express approval of the authorities. Such increases have in the past sometimes been conceded with the explicit purpose of facilitating the relevant industry's investment program by augmenting the volume of funds (retained earnings) available to it for "self-finance." In other instances the connection between price policy and the implementation of the Plan is less distinct.

In the nationalized sectors of industry, of course, the prices or rates automatically come under public control. But it is a question as to how far price policy in these sectors may be said to have been used to further the objectives of the Plan. In the whole public sector the price and rates policy has often been governed by the purpose of keeping down the cost-of-living index as a way of combatting inflation. In the private sector too, price controls, imposed from time to time on certain specified goods or services, or—as under the stabilization program launched in September 1963—on practically all commodities, have been similarly motivated. The link with the Plans, as opposed to the stabilization programs, is remote.

The quantitative or physical controls, which were important in the early years of the Monnet Plan, are at present few. Some of them specifically concern the oil companies, this sector being one where the government reserves to itself special rights of supervision and intervention. Thus permits are required for opening new refineries and (since 1963) for expanding old ones. Of general application is the building permit, required for almost all construction of both business premises and residential housing. Its main purpose up till now, however, has been that of enforcing certain building and urban planning rules. But it is possible, under a new regulation, that it may in the future be used to "guide" the regional distribution of new industrial development. More "selective" in its application, so far as the Plan is concerned, has been the special installation permit required, since 1956, for new plants and plant extensions of more than a certain size in the Paris area, with the object of promoting industrial decentralization. This requirement has more recently been extended to offices.

It is supposed to be characteristic of "soft" planning, however, that it relies for its implementation not so much on physical restraints and prohibitions, or authoritarian directives, as on priority allocations of investment funds, and on fiscal and financial incentives.

Public Investments and Investments Financed Out of Public Funds

A large part of France's gross fixed investments are still financed out of public funds, provided by the Treasury under various headings of the budget. In recent years the proportion has been a little less than a quarter.[1] The proportion was very much higher in the years of the Monnet Plan. From 54 percent in 1947 it rose to 64 percent in 1949, which was the maximum. In 1951-52 it still amounted to 41 percent. By 1956 it had dropped to 25 percent; and it has varied little from this level since.

In 1961 the total figure for gross fixed investments financed out of Treasury funds was approximately 13,000 million NF. Of this total some 5,000 million NF related to investments made directly by the State and to investment grants made by it to the local authorities. By far the larger part was public investment of the traditional kind, i.e., in "social fixed capital." Another 3,800 million NF went to the financing of the "national enterprises." Out of the remaining 4,600 million, housing took 2,800 million, most of it going to the semi-public HLM (or "moderate rent housing") organisms. Private "industry, trade and tourism" took less than 700 million (over 200 of it still under the heading of "war damage"), and farming about 800 million. The major part of the State financing of investments of the national enterprises [2] and of private industry takes place through a special Treasury account called the "Fund for Economic and Social Development" (FDES). This was established in its present form in 1955, but had a predecessor, set up in connection with the Monnet Plan.

If we consider the total of "public investments" in the sense of all those made directly by the State and the local authorities, *plus* all those made by the nationalized

---

[1] The figures are taken from the Annual Report of the Fund for Economic and Social Development (FDES).

[2] The "national enterprises" which draw finance from the Treasury (FDES) are the following:
   a) Fuel and power sector: Atomic Energy Commission, French Coal Authority, French Electricity Authority, French Gas Authority, the National Company of the Rhone (electricity), Gas of the South-West.
   b) Transport sector: French National Railways (SNCF), Paris Transport Authority (RATP), Paris Airport, Air France.
Other national enterprises (in the manufacturing sector), such as the Renault Motor Works and Sud Aviation (aeroplanes), do not depend on the FDES. State financing of the Post and Telecommunications (PTT) does not come under it either. Treasury funds going to these concerns come under other headings of the budget.

and other public enterprises (including what they finance not only out of Treasury funds but also by direct borrowing on the market or out of retained earnings) the proportion of these investments to the country's total gross fixed investments reaches about 35 percent. If we add to these "public investments" the private investments financed out of public funds, the proportion comes to well over 40 percent.

What we are chiefly observing here, however, is what a large part of investments is controlled by the public authorities in any modern economy (with or without a "Plan") in which to the already large amount of "traditional" public activities, are added a number of important nationalized industries and enterprises. Even among the so-called "productive" fixed investments (exclusive, that is, of investments in housing) of "enterprises" alone, the proportion accounted for by *public* enterprises was in France about 35 percent on the average during the three years 1959-61.[3] In such circumstances the public authorities exert a big influence, also, on the privately-run

firms from which they purchase their supplies, and of whom they may in some instances be the chief customer.

The FDES makes its loans under three different procedures, according to the class of borrower. Loans to the national enterprises are made directly through the Treasury. Those to the big "basic" industries in the private sector are granted as individual loans to the firms concerned on the responsibility of the FDES, but with the Crédit National, the big semi-public industrial credit institute, acting as intermediary. Finally, loans to firms in other parts of the private sector are made to those firms by the Crédit National or other intermediaries, acting this time on their own responsibility, out of funds allocated to them by the Treasury *en bloc* for the relevant category of borrowers. The loans are long term (i.e., for periods of over five years) , and they are made at interest rates which vary according to the borrower and the operations, but which have generally been perceptibly below the rate which the same borrower would have had to pay on the

---

[3] The figures are taken from the national income accounts.

market. Obviously the FDES can, through its Board of Directors and its several Committees, on all of which the Commissariat au Plan is represented, see that there is conformity with the aims of the Plan both in the nature of the investments, public or private, that are financed out of public funds, and in the order of priority in which borrowers are accommodated.

In the earlier postwar years, and particularly at the time of the Monnet Plan, the Treasury (or the Fund which was the FDES's predecessor) was a principal source of finance for the basic industries in the private sector, and most especially for the steel industry. It had been important, still, under the 2nd Plan. But the 3rd Plan [4] announced the government's intention of henceforth reducing the proportion of investments financed out of Treasury funds and of encouraging private financing. In 1958 the FDES stopped making new loans to the basic industries

in the private sector; in 1959 it again made none; and in each of the three years 1960-62 it granted only a very small amount (mostly to the chemical industry). While the FDES remained a major (though not the only) source of investment finance for the national enterprises in the fuel and power and the transport sectors, its role as a lender to *private* industry was now small. The FDES [5] roughly estimated that in 1960-61 the proportion of gross investments in the sector of "private industry, commerce and tourism" financed out of public funds (loans and grants) was not much more than 4 percent.

Treasury Aid to Private Industry

The bulk of the finance provided by the Fund to this sector now goes to three categories: first, "small and medium enterprises" and artisans; secondly, the hotel industry; [6] and thirdly, larger industrial firms engaging in operations of conversion, regrouping (concentration and specialization),

---

[4] *Op. cit.*, pp. 44 ff.

[5] 8th Annual Report (p. 810 in *Statistiques et Etudes Financières,* Supplement, June 1963).

[6] The loans are granted through the Caisse centrale de Crédit hôtelier, commercial et industriel to "small and medium industries," and through the Chambre syndicale des Banques populaires to individual artisans. Loans to the larger firms go through the Crédit National already mentioned, or through the Caisse des Dépôts (see footnote 16 p. 46 below).

and decentralization, and in other operations conducing to regional development. Relatively little of the finance now goes to private industry under other headings than these. Intervention by the State to help private industry to finance itself has not, however, been confined to the provision of cheap loan capital. To the third category mentioned above it also makes outright grants, or "equipment premia," or loans and premia combined. Sometimes it has undertaken to cover part of the interest charges on funds borrowed by the firm directly on the capital market, thus putting these in effect on a par, so far as interest charges are concerned, with the "cheap" Treasury loans; but recourse to this practice has declined in recent years. The State may also give its guarantee in order to enable bonds to be issued on the capital market more easily or more cheaply; but recently this practice, too, has been little used, except in connection with bonds issued by the Regional Development Companies,[7] which also benefit from a government guarantee of a minimum dividend for their shareholders.

On the whole the tendency since 1958 has been to reduce the volume of direct aid from the State to industry through the FDES, and to encourage firms to obtain their finance as far as possible, through regular market channels, or from the Regional Development Companies. Even the category "conversion and decentralization, etc.," received in 1960-62 only a small and declining volume of loan finance. The "special equipment premia" for encouraging regional development were in those years more important than State loans or than borrowings (from private sources) on which the State undertook to bear part of the interest charges.

Thus direct State participation in the financing of private industry was now of only marginal significance. Like a number of other items of government policy, its use in the past had been dictated in large part by the abnormal conditions on the French capital market, conditions of which one of the

---

[7] The purpose of these companies, which have been established under a law of 1955, and of which 21 (covering all areas of France except the Paris Region) existed by the end of 1962, is to provide medium- and long-term capital for the smaller firms which cannot make direct capital issues on the market. The chief means of providing such finance has been the (State-guaranteed) group loan issue.

causes was a long history of inflation.

Qualitative Controls Over Capital Issues and Credit

The planning authorities have, however, other ways of influencing the volume and direction of investments in the private sector. One is via selective controls over capital issues, over long-term borrowing from the three big semi-public credit institutes (Crédit National, Crédit Foncier and Crédit Agricole),[8] and over medium-term borrowing from the banks.

Since 1946 the Minister of Finance has had authority to exercise control over all medium and large issues (those over 25 million old francs)[9] of shares and debentures. The control actually exercised has, however, varied greatly in strictness, according to the conditions on the capital market. Originally the control meant that the dossier relating to the proposed issue, and presented by the applicant's bank, had to be examined by a special committee at the Ministry of Fi-

nance for its "economic interest," and the Ministry's authorization, if given, indicated the date at which the issue might be made. After the Monnet Plan was over, and as conditions on the capital market improved, the authorities proceeded in 1954-55 progressively to simplify the formalities until the control no longer entailed any prior examination of the investment project's economic merits but only the fixing of an issue date compatible with the possibilities of the market.

The inflationary situation of 1957-58, however, caused stricter controls to be reintroduced. The Ministry of Finance called attention to the necessity in this situation of giving priority to the financing of investments that would contribute towards making the country "independent with respect to fuel and power" and towards improving its foreign trade balance by increasing exports and decreasing imports. These were the same investment categories as had been placed at the top of the list of priorities by the 3rd Plan.[10] It was

---

[8] The first dealing mostly with industrial credit, the second with real estate credit, and the third with farm credit.

[9] See footnote 10 on p. 21 above.

[10] *Op. cit.,* pp. 10, 50.

now required that all *large* share issues (i.e., those of 100 million old francs and above) should obtain a specific authorization from the Ministry, and this meant submitting a dossier containing precise information concerning the nature of the investment envisaged, and, particularly, the company's present position and future prospects in the export market.[11] For bonds the control was more severe than for shares. Even medium-sized bond issues (i.e., those between 25 and 100 million old francs) had to be brought to the notice of the Minister, who might require the terms to be modified or the date to be postponed; while for large issues (those of 100 million old francs and above) the rule was the same as for shares.

With the progress towards financial rehabilitation in the second half of 1958 and the early months of 1959, however, the regulations were again relaxed, so far as share issues were concerned. The rule for these now was that large issues merely had to be brought to the notice of the Minister of Finance, and that he might ask for their

postponement. For bonds the stricter rules were retained. This distinction was dictated by one of the abnormal features of the capital market, namely the tendency for the bond market to be generally poorly supplied with funds in relation to the demand, and for the situation on the share market to be the other way round.

The three big specialized public or semi-public credit institutes mentioned above, and some smaller ones, make long-term loans, i.e., loans for terms of over five years, and usually between ten and twenty years, not only out of advances from the FDES but also, and mostly, out of non-Treasury funds (their own resources together with funds raised on the capital market). It is with these loans out of non-Treasury funds that we shall now be concerned.

A rule has existed for a number of years that the Crédit National should grant large loans (for amounts exceeding 2.5 million NF) only for financing investment programs that have been approved by the Commissariat au Plan. This has meant, as the National Credit

---

[11] For companies engaging in prospecting for, exploiting, and transforming oil and natural gas, the regulation applied to medium as well as large issues (i.e., to all issues above 25 million old francs).

Council [12] reports, that these long-term industrial loans are in large part reserved for the finance of equipment programs that are in conformity with the Plan. Up until 1958-59 most of these long-term loans were granted at rates of interest below the market level, the State assuming part of the burden of the interest charges, or else giving a guarantee. This meant that funds borrowed from this source were similar, as regards costs to the borrower, to those obtained out of Treasury funds. In 1960, however, the practice of subsidizing interest rates was used much less frequently, and in 1961 it was almost abandoned,[13] so that by this time the long-term loans were being made at rates close to the market rates. And, as we have seen the FDES was then making practically no new loans to the big "basic" industries in the private sector. These changes were part of the process of the gradual withdrawal of the Treasury as lender, guarantor, and subsidizer of loans, except in special cases.

One important factor which had altered during this period was the receptiveness of the capital market to new issues of securities. Even on the bond market there had been a big improvement since the measures of financial rehabilitation of 1958-59. Thus the yield on "classical-type" (i.e., non-indexed) bonds of private companies had fallen from an average of about 8.3 percent in 1957-58 to 6.6 in 1961, and 6.5 in 1962.[14] The yield on "indexed" or "participating" bonds [15] of such companies had fallen from 7.5 percent in 1957-58 to 5.8 in 1961, and 5.6 in 1962. The yields on government

---

[12] The Conseil National du Crédit, which was set up in December 1945, at the time of the bank nationalizations, as a body (comprising representatives of government departments, the Bank of France, the banks, and business) with the task of directing credit policy.

[13] Cf. The Annual Reports of the National Credit Council.

[14] The cost to the borrower making new issues on the market was, of course, perceptibly higher than these figures indicate. The costs of issue, taxes, etc., would add perhaps another 2 percent.

[15] "Indexed" bonds are those for which the money value of the capital or the interest varies with some index of changes in the price level or in the value of money (e.g., the price of gold on the free market, the index of the prices of securities, including shares, quoted on the Stock Exchange, or the price of the product or service sold by the issuing company). "Participating" bonds are those which give the holder a share in the growth of revenue from sales or in the distributed profits of the company. Many indexed and participating bonds had been issued in the 1950's as a way of giving the otherwise reluctant subscriber a hedge against inflation.

bonds, and on the bonds of the public and semi-public enterprises had fallen correspondingly.

Medium-term lending (for 1-5 years) is mainly the province of the commercial banks. The loans give rise to bills that are rediscountable at the public or semi-public credit institutions (usually the Caisse des Dépôts [16] in the case of industrial loans) or at the Bank of France. And as part of the procedure involved in making them eligible for rediscount, they are subject to previous authorization and signature by one of these institutions (the Crédit National when they are industrial loans), one of the examiners of the relevant dossier being an official of the Bank of France. The checking of these loans for "conformity with the Plan" has in the past been much looser than that over long-term loans, although the larger ones (of 1 million NF and over) might be referred to the Commissariat and scrutinized for such conformity.

The Uncontrolled Sources of Finance

What had—so far at least—remained definitely and at all times beyond the control of the planning authorities were, first, investments out of the firms' own resources (retained earnings plus depreciation allowances), and secondly, investments financed by short-term bank credit. Even the big nationalized banks did not, until 1963 at least, apply qualitative controls to short-term loans. This was a fact which many planners regarded as a lost opportunity. Some of them think, too, that self-finance by industry ought to be regulated.

How big have these uncontrolled items been? The FDES estimates that "self-finance" (out of retained earnings and depreciation allowances) has accounted in recent years (1959-62) for not far from 40 percent of total gross *fixed* investments in the economy. In the years 1956-58 it had represented a still larger proportion (probably close

[16] The Caisse des Dépôts et Consignations is an institution at which the Caisse National d'Epargne and the ordinary savings banks redeposit the greater part of their customers' savings deposits. The Caisse des Dépôts' traditional activity on the lending side was that of financing the local authorities. It now lends to the HLM offices and subscribes to new bond issues of the central government, the national enterprises, and public credit institutions.

to 45 percent). Looking at the figures for all long, medium, and short-term loans outstanding [17] to enterprises and individuals (i.e., excluding local authorities), we observe the following proportions. Long-term loans, over which the control for "conformity with the Plan" was tightest, accounted in 1960-61 for 41-42 percent of the total medium-term loans, over which the control was looser, for 16-17 percent, and short-term loans, over which there was (then at least) no control, for 41 percent.[18]

We should notice, however, that of the medium-term credits about 40 percent consisted of the "special construction loans" for housing, and that not far from 50 percent of the long-term credits were also housing loans (mostly to the HLM). Reference has been made already to the French government's big role in the housing field. In 1961 out of France's total gross fixed investments of 55.1 billion NF, residential construction accounted for 12.3 billion (or about 22 percent). No less than 90 percent of the total number of housing units constructed (316,000) were, in this as in previous years, State-aided in one way or another (special construction loans, construction premia, loans and premia combined, contributions towards interest charges). That the State aids almost all the housing built is again one of the legacies of past economic policy: in this instance inflation combined with rent control.

The Selective Bank Lending Policy Solicited in September 1963

A new development, looking towards greater selectivity in the distribution of bank credit, including for the first time short-term credit, took place in connection with the government's stabilization plan of September 1963. The banks were asked (not ordered) to follow a selective policy, in respect of all their lending (short- and medium-term), for two purposes. One was that of aiding the fight against inflation. The banks were advised to reject applications for loans from those intending to use the funds for specula-

---

[17] Included are those granted out of funds provided directly or indirectly by the Treasury and those granted by the various financial institutions out of non-Treasury funds.

[18] The total of all the loans (short, medium, and long) outstanding was 114 billion NF at the end of 1960 and 135 billion at the end of 1961.

tive purchases of raw materials, etc., and to give specially favorable consideration to industrial and commercial borrowers wanting to finance investments that were likely to reduce costs and prices, or desiring to set up or expand business in areas where labor was abundant. The second purpose was that of favoring borrowers who respected the aims of the Plan. The directives given under this second head will be mentioned later.

We lack information as to how successful this attempt to persuade the banks to exercise generalized qualitative credit control has been.

Fiscal Instruments: General Reforms

The 4th Plan, in a section entitled "The Means of Action," devotes a chapter to "Fiscal Means." Speaking of what must be done in the tax field to permit the realization of the aims of the Plan, it mentions first the task of taking measures of fiscal policy that will favor economic growth, and especially of eliminating certain features of the existing tax system

which hinder such growth. It points to the importance in this connection, as the 3rd Plan had done before it, of proceeding further with the efforts already made in France to achieve *neutrality* of the tax system as between different branches of activity and different forms of business organization. For non-neutrality meant that intrinsically less profitable lines of production, or less efficient forms of organization, might frequently be chosen in preference to the more profitable or efficient ones, merely because the tax system discriminated in their favor.

A big step towards neutrality had already been taken in the indirect tax field by the reforms of 1954-55. The chief consequence of these was to substitute, in most cases, the tax on value added (TVA),[19] at the rate of normally 20 percent, for the old indirect taxes (or taxes on expenditure), including the general turnover tax. This had had the disadvantage of being cumulative (or "cascading") from one sales stage to another. It had thus discriminated in favor

---

[19] The object of the TVA is to hit only the value which the firm concerned has "added" to the products it sells, and not the value of materials, investment goods, services, etc., which it has used in production (or selling), and which have already been charged with the tax when sold by their producers, wholesalers, etc.

of branches of production or forms of organization of production that were more highly integrated as against those that were less so. An important reminder here is that indirect taxes (the TVA and other indirect taxes levied for the benefit either of the central or of the local government authorities) still constitute a very large part of total tax revenues in France (about 60 percent compared with roughly 25 percent in the United States). Though some of the initial exceptions to the generalized application of the TVA had been removed by early 1959, there remained, as the 4th Plan remarked, some sectors which were exempt, or else subject to indirect taxes calculated on other than a value-added basis, to which the government intended to extend it in the near future. The TVA does not, for example, yet apply to the general run of retail businesses.

Among the countries of the Common Market, all of them dependent on a high proportion of indirect taxation by U.S. standards, France was, however, the one which had gone furthest towards substituting the TVA for other forms. At the Brussels headquarters of EEC it was being recommended that the whole Community of the Six should follow this course in its approach towards a common tax system.

Another task which the 4th Plan saw as still remaining in the French quest for tax neutrality, was a more complete elimination of double taxation of the earnings of mother companies and their affiliates. In respect of the companies tax—normally chargeable at 50 percent of both distributed and undistributed profits [20]—there was still an element of double taxation, which constituted an obstacle to those continual structural adjustments (creation of new industrial ensembles, concentration and specialization of productive activities, creation of associations for scientific and technical research, etc.) which modern conditions impose, and in which France had lagged behind in the past.

Reforming the tax system in this direction of increased neutrality may be considered an instrument of the Plan, insofar as it helps remove obstacles to economic growth. It is, however, an instrument which

---

[20] But see pp. 50-51 below.

any country suffering from the same type of "unneutrality" might have used as a means of promoting economic expansion, whether or not it had French planning. And much the same may be said about another tax reform introduced in 1960 to give general encouragement to investment activity. This is the measure allowing firms to opt for the diminishing balance method of calculating depreciation on industrial and other equipment [21] in place of the previous straight-line method. In introducing this measure France was doing what had already been done earlier in some other countries, notably West Germany.

Selective Tax Treatment

The adoption of fiscal policy measures such as these cannot be regarded as especially characteristic of French planning. Much more so are the measures which are "selective" as between one activity (which "conforms" to the aims of the Plan) and another (which does not "conform").

One kind of tax relief, supposed to be selective in this sense and obtainable since 1957, relates to new share issues by companies which can show that they are "contributing to the realization of the objects of the Plan" or towards the "programs for regional action." In such cases exemption from the companies tax for seven years is granted in respect of dividends of up to 5 percent paid on the new capital. Although the by now customary phrase regarding "conformity with the Plan" was used, the main purpose of this measure seems to have been to encourage firms to borrow more largely on the equities market.[22] The exemption is another instance of measures aimed at helping to relieve the abnormal situation on the capital market. As the 4th Plan noted, it also responded, in a limited degree (especially since it related only to new issues), to the desire of many people to make it a general rule that the rate of the companies tax should be lower on distributed than on undistributed profits (as is already the case in West Germany), the object being to encourage companies to pay out more of their profits to share-

---

[21] The provision was extended in 1962 to light industrial buildings.

[22] Cf. Conseil National du Crédit, Annual Report for 1960 (p. 160), and for 1961 (p. 162).

holders and in this way to feed more of them on to the capital market. This measure might thus be considered as another attempt to introduce increased rationality, by some people's lights at least, into the tax system. And even if only partial as yet in application, it might, if these views prevailed, become general in the future. In that case it would cease to be "selective" from the planning standpoint.

The 4th Plan did, however, stress the point—and here it differed from the 3rd Plan where the emphasis was on "neutrality"—that the tax system may "go beyond neutrality" and "play a selective role favoring certain operations . . . judged to be particularly interesting by the Plan." It also noted that within the present juridical and administrative set-up in France "the fiscal lever figures among the most important means of inducement at the disposal of the public authorities." It observed nonetheless that the use of this instrument for the purpose described was rather a new thing, and needed cautious handling. Otherwise it might eat into the tax base, or contravene the principle that the tax system should be simple.

The Plan distinguished two ways in which fiscal policy may be used expressly to encourage the realization of the Plan. The first method, as it said, is composed of the relatively familiar fiscal means of intervention which apply all over the system, or else are selective by branch. The greater part of these were already in place, it said, and new inducements of the kind would be used in a strictly limited number of cases "in favor of the realization of the objectives of the 4th Plan which are the most difficult to reach."

The Plan referred to two items under the first head. One was differential rates of indirect taxation. (Such are the reduced rates of the TVA applying to certain products used by farmers, and to certain foodstuffs of wide consumption, and the increased rates on certain luxury goods.) The other item was special depreciation formulas. Numerous special systems of accelerated depreciation (representing exceptions from the general rule of the straight-line method) had applied, prior to the Law of December 1959 (which authorized the general adoption of the diminishing-balance method), to particular industries, such as steel and mines, to firms doing a large export business, or to certain types of equipment. And a few new privileged cases were added after the 4th Plan came into force. Some of these special systems were considered more favorable than the new general one. All of them expire, however, at the beginning of 1965, which is the end of the transitional period during which the firms concerned might elect to keep them. This means that another "selective" planning instrument has been suppressed in the quest for tax neutrality.

The second kind of tax discrimination which the Plan distinguishes is that which takes place *at the level of the firm* (or sometimes group of firms). Under this heading fall the exemptions accorded "case by case" by the Minister of Finance. The Plan notes that there are 15 special exemption procedures in force, and that eight of them are of great interest for purposes of implementing the Plan.

One of the eight is the exemption, already mentioned, of dividends on new issues from the companies tax. A second important one is the reduction to a nominal figure of the still substantial (over

13 percent) tax (*droit de mutation*) on transfers of land and buildings intended for business use when these transfers are connected with industrial regroupings (concentration and specialization), or with the program for industrial decentralization and regional development. A third is the extension of the tax régime of "mother companies and affiliates" (*sociétés mères et filiales*) to cases which do not automatically qualify for it under the general rule as at present formulated, but which may under recent laws (of 1957 and 1959) be granted by special authorization in approved cases. The same régime may be extended to the companies formed to group the firms in a particular sector (e.g., shipbuilding and the steel, electrical equipment, and engineering industries) for the purpose of allowing these firms to make collective bond issues on the capital market instead of individual ones. A fourth kind of relief is the reduction of, or total exemption from, the business tax (*contribution de patente*) for commercial and industrial firms which help to promote regional development. This is a tax which is levied, at rates varying with the place and the type of business, for

the benefit of the local authorities. Other items of relief benefit companies formed by groups of firms for various purposes (such as carrying out activities in common in order to facilitate adaptation to the necessities of the European Common Market, constructing and using in common an industrial ensemble, or "converting and rationalizing"). In addition to the eight major exemption procedures the Plan lists three which are of interest to companies and institutions engaged in scientific and technical research.

The Plan remarks in defense of these forms of "selective" tax relief that their total incidence on the budget is "relatively small in absolute amount and not anything like comparable with the increase in tax revenues resulting each year from the expansion of the national product." There is, however, another possible ground for objection —which has not gone entirely unnoticed in France—namely that the "case by case" treatment, as opposed to the "same rule for all," may become arbitrary in the granting of privileges and favors, and lead to other abuses.

It is customary to speak of all these items of tax relief as special

facilities granted in approved cases —those that are in conformity with the objectives of the Plan. But some of them are probably destined in the end to become automatically applicable to all cases in the wake of a tax reform aimed at removing obstacles to *general economic expansion*. They would in that event cease to be instruments for imposing the *more specific* aims of the Plan.

Procedures and Negotiations

Certain of the special concessions concerning taxation are, the 4th Plan tells us, of a semi-automatic character, only those applications being turned down that are devoid of any real economic interest. In other cases, however, the procedure now usually followed is that of the "fiscal contract" in which the government grants a firm the privileged tax treatment in return for a certain *quid pro quo* consisting of specified operations which it is thought necessary to encourage as a way of achieving the objectives of the Plan. Or perhaps all firms in a particular branch may be covered by an agreement with the relevant trade association.

The fiscal contract is one form of the "quasi-contract," a procedure first mentioned by this name in the Interim Plan presented in the spring of 1960, but which had earlier antecedents. The quasi-contract may be used to establish the financial facilities (prompt access to funds, cheap loans, equipment premia, etc.) which the State undertakes to grant in order to aid a certain investment program. This procedure seems to have been conceived as a way of making it easier for firms to take advantage of the "big potential" of incentives allowed by the existing regulations, a potential which, the Interim Plan said, had not been fully exploited. Few such "contracts" have been signed so far, however.

The process of negotiating benefits, privileges, or price increases starts in some instances, as was noted earlier, at the stage of the Commission work. In a few cases the Commissions have in their written reports emphasized the facilities which they claim to need as a condition for implementing the Plan—instead of giving prime consideration to the more "objective" aspects of the latter.[23] This fact is deplored by some planning enthusiasts, who oppose an attitude tinged

with a certain amount of boy-scoutism to hard-headed business behavior.

Professor Bauchet remarks that the negotiation within the Commissions takes place most easily in the sectors containing only a few firms; and that more generally the "dialogue with the public authorities," at whatever stage it takes place, is closer in the basic sectors or in the sectors where the units are large, than in the general run of manufacturing industries.[24] This is doubtless one reason why some critics of the Plan, as it is at present organized, accuse it of working mostly to the benefit of monopoly groups. On the other hand, it is also the big firms that are most likely to be hit by strict controls over capital issues, long- and medium-term credit, etc.

No Penalties for Non-Conformers

The Plan may grant or withhold favors, and may perhaps revoke those once given, according as a firm is, or is not, making investments "in conformity with the Plan." But it does not directly penalize an industry, or the firms in it, because that industry has under-

---

[23] Cf. Bauchet, *op. cit.*, pp. 64-65 and p. 171.
[24] *Ibid.*, pp. 102 and 240.

or over-shot the "target" assigned to it in the Plan. It does not apply sanctions for failure to comply with its objectives. Doing this would mean "coercive" instead of "indicative" planning. There is no binding obligation on any industry—or on the firms belonging to it—to reach the targets set for the branch or sub-branch, and no targets are set for individual firms as opposed to whole branches or sub-branches.

VII.

THE EXTENT TO WHICH THE INSTRUMENTS ARE USED AND THE NOTION OF CONFORMITY

No systematic account is publicly available of the frequency with which the various planning instruments have been used or of the motivation of their use in the individual cases. Only for the item "industrial conversion, decentralization and regional development programs" is the information fairly full. Except in this instance we do not know how many firms, and in what branches, obtained special facilities, large or small, for doing something that was "in conformity with the Plan," and which they might or might not have done without such facilities. Similarly, we do not know, how often it happened that a firm was prevented (by being refused access to funds) from making a desired investment on the grounds that the latter was "not in conformity with the Plan." Nor do we know (except again in the cases already noted) what sort of activity was, in the various instances, and at various times, held to be "in conformity," and what not. The available information about this whole aspect of French planning is scrappy.

One of the most explicit published statements on the subject of "conformity," as it was being considered at the particular date, consists of the directives given to the banks in the autumn of 1963 in connection with the authorities' request that they should follow a selective lending policy, aimed both at combatting inflation and at "respecting the aims of the Plan." In this latter connection the banks were asked to favor three types of operation. The first was the modernization of businesses which were under strong pressure from foreign competition (the banks being provided with a confidential list for their guidance). The second was investment by firms that were endeavoring to expand exports. The

third was operations for strengthening the productive structure, e.g., by regroupings of producing units leading to greater concentration and specialization. This, as we have already had occasion to notice, is a process which other planning instruments were expressly designed to aid.

The above directives were, it is true, much influenced by the situation of the moment, which was one of financial crisis. It is fairly certain, however, that promotion of exports even in other situations has been a frequent *quid pro quo* for the "special favors." It was, as indicated previously, one of the qualifications for obtaining access to the capital market during the critical period in 1957-58, for having the right to apply accelerated depreciation formulas, and so on.[1]

Perhaps we do not go wrong if we sum up the broad characteristics of the mode of application of the Plan to the private sector of the economy in the following points:

1. The planning authorities have sought to influence the actions of

---

[1] See also the examples of the use (up to 1961) of financial and fiscal aids to encourage exports cited by Maurice Niveau, "La Planification indicative en France," *Economie Appliquée,* 1962.

the individual economic operators partly by using the "stick" (e.g., refusal of access to the capital market or to long and medium-term credit, or placing at the back of the queue for funds) and partly by distributing special "carrots" (direct and indirect subsidies, and other favors).

2. Generally speaking the stick was in times of "good weather" used only very lightly, "conformity with the Plan" then being very broadly interpreted to include any activity serving general economic development. In "bad weather" (financial stringency, inflation, balance-of-payments difficulties), of which France has had a good deal, "conformity" was interpreted more narrowly, and the stick used more, and sometimes very, heavily. Almost always sure of escaping from its rap were branches, or firms, doing a large export business, and those producing goods for home consumption that were in strong competition with imports. We may observe that the criterion for establishing priority of access to funds has here been not very dissimilar from that adopted in other countries, which have, in difficult times, limited that access in the name not of "French planning" but of "general economic policy."

3. A special stick, as we saw, has been used on firms desiring to set up or expand in the Paris area. But again this is not something without a parallel in recent years in "non-planning" countries (e.g., Britain).

4. The same activities that got no, or only light, use of the stick also got a lot of the "carrots." While in the earlier years it was the "basic" industries which got most of these, the emphasis shifted later (after 1955) to the category of activities referred to as "industrial regroupings, decentralization, and regional development." These have, as we saw, specially-labeled carrots assigned to them. The decentralization and regional development program has, however, not been as successful as had been hoped and expected. Among the activities eligible for the other assistance, export expansion has again constantly occupied an important place. (The direct subsidization of exports is, we should remember, forbidden to France and to her partners in the European Common Market since 1959 by the Rome Treaty.) Other activities that are explicitly indicated as being eligible are scientific and technical re-

search, and the launching of new products. Once more we notice that some of the activities which the Plan has most clearly sought to encourage (e.g., export expansion, regional development, research) are among those which other countries, without planning, have also aided. But again, in many of the cases where carrots are distributed, "general economic development" may be as near as we can come to defining what "conformity with the Plan" means.

5. The instrumentation of the Plan has not since 1959 at least been closely geared to the attainment of *sectoral* targets. It has not, that is to say, been very selective as between different branches of the economy, but has served rather to favor certain activities common to a great many branches.

6. Few small firms have been affected in either good or bad weather by stick or carrots.

7. Even some of the larger ones have been little and seldom affected (except by the export incentives) in certain circumstances: (a) if they could largely rely on self-finance out of retained earnings, and could get along without much long- or medium-term finance from outside sources; and (b) if they pre-ferred to do without special aids, as for example when they chose an unsubsidized location for their industrial expansion instead of a subsidized one, because it was more profitable to do so.

We cannot, however, put these characteristics of the method of implementing the Plan into figures. And we cannot judge how great an influence the planning instruments have had in effectively steering the course of economic events in the "right" direction, or away from that which it would have followed "spontaneously."

The Changing Nature of the Instruments

Looking at the history of the way in which the planning instruments have evolved, we notice certain marked shifts in emphasis from one Plan to another. Under the Monnet Plan the instruments were, as already remarked, those of "hard" planning. The 2nd Plan, or the first of the "soft" Plans, relied heavily on the control over investment finance, of which a large part, even for the private sector, still came out of funds provided by the Treasury.

The 3rd Plan envisaged, and expressly recommended, a shift away from this system, i.e., a reduction in the proportion of investments financed out of public funds, and an increase in the proportion financed out of private funds. It spoke of the desirability of doing everything possible to reestablish normally functioning capital and money markets. It is true that it foresaw the continued necessity both for the State to aid some parts of the private sector with loan guarantees, interest-rate subsidies, and other grants, and for it to direct the private funds towards investments in accordance with a system of priorities. However, such direction was conceived as a temporary expedient, the need for which would pass once savings became abundant enough (which was not then, i.e., in 1957, it remarked, an immediate prospect) to allow all "profitable projects," as it was put, to be financed.[2]

By the time that the 4th Plan was in preparation, considerable progress had, as noted, been made towards strengthening the capital market, and leaving firms to borrow at the market rates of interest. And what we find in this Plan, therefore, is an emphasis, not found in the previous Plans, on the use of fiscal incentives as implementation. But even these were of uncertain duration. The Minister of Finance, commenting in June 1962 on the fiscal incentives that would be used to facilitate the realization of the priority aims of the Plan, repeated what had already been indicated in the Text of the 4th Plan, that it was the desire of the government to arrive at "generalized tax harmonization and neutrality." He said that the incentives should preferably take the form of direct subsidies (government contributions towards interest charges, or capital grants) rather than of tax exemption. But again we should recall that since France has become a member of the European Common Market, there are certain limitations, imposed by the Rome Treaty, on the extent to which she may resort to direct subsidies.

We thus reach this conclusion. As the task, encouraged by the Plans themselves, of restoring normally functioning financial and other markets went successfully forward, the Plan lost a good part of its instruments, so that, if it was

---

[2] Cf. Text of the 3rd Plan, p. 50.

to remain a "real" Plan, it had to look for others. Or, to put it another way, the succession of steps taken ever since 1948 towards the rehabilitation of the market economy had little by little dissolved "soft planning" into "economic liberalism." France was slower than other countries in restoring market mechanisms after the War, but has nevertheless moved persistently in this direction. The deviation (reintroduction of price controls, and of strict controls over the access to funds) which took place in 1963-64 was connected with the stabilization program—not with the 4th Plan—and was intended to last only so long as stability was in danger. As Mr. Georges Pompidou, the Prime Minister, promised in March 1964: "The moment will come when from the present *dirigisme* we shall revert to liberalism."

The "Mystique" of the Plan

It is not surprising, then, that to many French planners the present apparatus for implementing the Plan appears inadequate. It is doubtless one of the inherent contradictions of "soft" planning, as opposed to "harder" varieties, that this should be so.

On the other hand, some of the planners maintain that, though the instruments seem too weak, the effectiveness of the Plan is greater than this circumstance might suggest. They attach great importance to its "psychological effect," to the power of suggestion and persuasion which it exerts at least over many of those numerous persons who participate in its preparation. The 2nd Plan, speaking of the method of general consultation of which it was the product, remarked that "very often action results from the consultation itself." [3] It was very largely in these terms that the father of French planning, and inventor of the Commissions system, Jean Monnet, originally saw his invention. "He was convinced," says Mr. Massé,[4] "that by working on the Plan those who would have to carry it out would spontaneously see that it was carried out. In this way the government's intervention during the execution of the Plan would not need to be heavy. Experience confirmed that

---

[3] *Ibid.*, p. 9.
[4] "French Methods of Planning," *Journal of Industrial Economics*, November 1962, p. 4.

he was right," Mr. Massé assures us.

It was this conception of Monnet's that laid the foundations of the philosophy of the so-called "concerted economy," a philosophy which has since won a big following in France. Referring to this aspect, Mr. Wickham tells us that: "The indicative plan implies a new sort of informal agreement . . . among autonomous decision-making centers (government agencies, public enterprises, private firms). Each of them commits itself morally (that is, unless it explicit-ly notifies the other parties) to carry out its share of the investment financed by means mentioned in the plan." [5] Some of the planners also lay emphasis on the Plan's "power as a myth," [6] and seriously suggest that it exerts an important part of its influence by this means.

These claims concerning the psychological and mystical influences of the Plan, and the morally binding obligations which it creates, are rightly viewed by many observers, both inside and outside France, with skepticism.

---

[5] *Op. cit.*, pp. 340-41.
[6] Cf. J. Fourastié and J. P. Courthéoux, *La Planification en France,* 1963, pp. 115-16, 139-40.

VIII.

COMPARISON OF FORECASTS
WITH ACTUAL PERFORMANCE

Comparisons between the targets or forecasts of the Plans and the results actually achieved have been made in the (since 1952) annual reports on the execution of the successive Plans. A summary comparison has been included, since the 2nd Plan, in the text of the following Plan. In approaching comparisons of this kind, an awareness is necessary of certain difficulties of a technical and methodological character. I shall refer to only some of these here.

Methodological Difficulties

1. We do not know exactly what items among the Plan's figures are meant to be "firm targets," which the Plan actively aims at reaching, and what are "mere forecasts" of what is likely to happen "spon-

taneously." As already remarked, no consistently clear distinction has been made between the two. In this section we shall, however, be as much interested in the one as the other. For the forecasts are themselves supposed to be a very important part of the Plan (conceived as a means of reducing uncertainty for the economic operators), and one way of judging its "efficacy" is by the accuracy of its forecasting. For the time being, therefore, I shall use the terms target and forecast as though they were interchangeable, reserving for later treatment the problems raised by the attempt, or what is for some planners the necessity, to distinguish between them.

2. Certain facts about the timetable of the preparation of the Plan must be kept in mind. In the case of the 4th Plan, for example, 1959 was the latest possible "reference" date which the Commissariat could use in making its preliminary forecasts for 1965, for the 28 branches, and for the broad categories of the national income accounts, which it passed to the Modernization Commissions in 1960. The Commissions had to make

their detailed forecasts by branch and sub-branch on the same "reference base"; and the final synthesis, or adding up of these forecasts to form the national aggregates (gross domestic product and its uses) was also initially made on this base. For the 2nd Plan the reference year 1952 had been used, and for the 3rd generally 1956, but in some instances 1957, and for agriculture 1954.

In reality, then, the forecasting for the terminal year of the 4th Plan was being made not over a four-year but over a six-year stretch. And by the time that the 4th Plan started even the data concerning past events, which the Commissions had used for making the detailed forecasts, were already two years old. In the final document of the Plan, however, both the big aggregates (of the national income tables) and the big sub-aggregates (for the nine broad sectors) [1] did appear on the base 1961. This was because, after the Commissions had completed their work, the Plan's statistical services interpolated provisional accounts for 1961,[2] between the accounts for 1959 and those for 1965. The final acounts for 1961

---

[1] See pp. 27-29 above.
[2] Cf. Commissariat au Plan, *Rapport sur l'Exécution du Plan en 1962 et 1963*, pp. 277-78.

were not, of course, available in the autumn when the Plan was submitted to the various superior authorities.

3. Both the 3rd and the 4th Plans' figures for the size and sectoral distribution of the labor force had to be based on the 1954 Census of Population data, and on estimates of changes after that. As we shall see below, there were big errors in these estimates.

4. In pluri-annual planning, whether the target of the Plan appears to have been reached or not can depend on chance occurrences in a single year, i.e., the terminal year of the Plan. It is only for this year that a precise target is set. For it is accepted that four-year (or six-year) forecasting cannot hope to anticipate exact rates of expansion—either for the big aggregates or for the narrower sub-aggregates —year by year, but must be content with the average rates for the entire four (or six) years. In such circumstances, if the rate of growth in the terminal year, but not in the preceding ones, happens to be

negative, cases may occur where it is a puzzle as to whether we should say that the Plan was fulfilled in the relevant branch or not. Cases of this kind are, of course, apt to be more frequent in agriculture than in industry. A noteworthy instance in industry was, however, that of automobile production in the terminal year of the 3rd Plan (1961). I shall refer to this again below.[3]

5. The comparison between the targets of forecasts of the Plans and the results actually achieved cannot be very rigorous, owing to the changing classifications in the statistics, the necessity of periodically revising the composition and weighting of index numbers,[4] and a certain vagueness in some of the definitions in the Plans. Most of these difficulties are inherent in the nature of economic measurement, and not a failing peculiar to French statistical methods.

6. The account given in one Plan of the results of the previous Plan is based on preliminary figures for the terminal year, the final figures

---

[3] See pp. 82-83.

[4] The recent revision of the index of industrial production is a good example. The old index had been compiled with weights appropriate to 1952. The new one adopted 1959 weights. The increase in industrial output between 1959 and 1962 appeared to be 25 percent on the basis of the old index, and only 22 percent on the basis of the new one.

not yet being available. For the final figures we need in many cases to refer to the Annual Reports on the Execution of the Plans, or to the regular publications of the National Institute of Statistics and Economic Studies (INSEE). Here we do not always find, ready made for us, the same groupings as were used by the Plan. On the other hand, the differences between the preliminary and the final figures are not always minimal. Some important instances will be mentioned in what follows. My remarks will be based on what appear to be the final figures.

7. There is at present no consensus of opinion as to how near the forecast should come to the realized results in order to be considered a "good" or "useful" forecast. All that we can say on this point is that planners are apt to apply more lenient standards than non-planners.

The Record

The 1st Plan (1947 to 1952-53), conceived at a time when national income accounting was still in its infancy, did not set an overall growth rate as one of its targets. Instead it set output or capacity targets for a number of basic industries and basic agricultural products, and indicated a figure for aggregate industrial production. The levels actually reached by 1952 were somewhat below the targets in the nationalized sectors of coal and electricity. They were well above for the volume of crude oil processed. They were well below for steel output, and above for cement. They were below for each of the four basic agricultural products (wheat, meat, milk, sugar). The year 1952 was, however, a time when disinflationary measures had to be taken, and when the rate of growth in the gross national product slowed down. It is usually said that the 1st Plan was actually realized with one year's delay, i.e., in 1953-54; but this is only as judged by the progress made in the basic sectors. In 1952, and also in 1953, the index of industrial production in the aggregate was not much more than 10 percent above the 1929 level, compared with the Plan's forecast of 25 percent. The year 1929 had been taken as the "reference year" in preference to 1938 because of the abnormally low level of activity which had prevailed in the French economy throughout the 1930's.

The reason for the big divergence between the target and the realization for industrial production as a whole was that most of the "non-basic" industries (i.e., the majority of manufacturing industries, in both producers' and consumers' goods sectors) still had very low output levels in 1952-53. Another task that had been postponed was that of remedying the housing shortage. In the three years 1950-52 the number of new housing units completed was only between 70 and 80 thousand a year. There was much discussion at the time concerning whether such a heavy concentration on the building up of the basic sectors was the right way of proceeding, or whether the consumer should have been given a break earlier.

The 2nd Plan (for 1954-57), benefiting from the progress made towards better national income accounting, was the first to set an overall growth rate for gross domestic output. The figure for the terminal year, of 25 percent above the 1952 level, was this time overreached, the growth actually registered being 29 percent. Industrial output rose to 45, instead of the projected 30, percent above the 1952 level. In the nationalized sectors, coal and gas were somewhat below the target, and electricity somewhat above. The volume of crude oil processed came about as far below the target this time (1957 was the year following the Suez crisis) as it had come above last time. Steel was at the target level, and chemicals greatly above. House building also exceeded the target figure. It was now running at a level much higher (162,000 units completed in 1954, rising to 274,-000 in 1957) than under the Monnet Plan, though still low in comparison with the huge backlog of needs. This time the "non-basic" manufacturing industries also made rapid progress, and in the aggregate their performance was more than equal to expectations. In agriculture some products (meat and milk) were at the target level, wheat was far above, and sugar below. Agricultural output in the aggregate was substantially below target level. Bad weather had intervened.

The figure for aggregate gross investment (inclusive of stocks) in 1957 was 41 percent above the 1952 level instead of the predicted 28 percent. It thus exceeded the target by much more than did either gross domestic production or private consumption. The deviations from target in individual sectors (here calculated from the figures for investment expenditures, at 1954 prices, during the entire four years 1954-57) in some cases followed the deviations of the output figures (as, for example, in the case of chemicals). But the whole group of "non-basic" manufacturing industries absorbed less capital than predicted, despite the larger increase in output. Particularly big deviations (nearly 30 percent) in excess of the target figures occurred in the sectors of housing and social equipment (schools and hospitals). The main reason (aside from the larger than expected number of houses built) was that building costs (calculated at 1954 prices) had been much higher than foreseen.

The success or "oversuccess" of the 2nd Plan was connected with the appearance in the last two of its four years of the inflation, and growing balance-of-payments difficulties (or large drawings on foreign exchange reserves and foreign credits), which provoked the financial crisis of 1958. This heritage from the 2nd Plan caused the 3rd Plan (1958-61) to start in very unfavorable conditions, and by the end of its second year (1959) it was one year behind schedule. In 1960 it was laid aside, and a new "Interim Plan" put in its place for the last two years. This plan set a target for gross domestic output in the terminal year (1961) 23 percent above the 1956 level in place of the 27 percent contained in the original 3rd Plan. It revised some of the subordinate objectives (notably that of exports) upwards, and others (including that for investments) downwards. In this way it succeeded in achieving for the growth in gross domestic output a remarkably close approximation between the (new) target and the actual result. Aggregate investments even came out equal to the initial target. In the nationalized industries of the power sector—the easiest sector for which to predict the demand though not always the supply—the "revised" targets, which were all equal to the "initial" targets except in the case of coal (for which a downward revision had been made), were all reached almost exactly. In the oil industry, too, the refining capacity grew as planned. For chemicals once again, and also for aluminum, the targets (though revised upwards in the Interim Plan) were surpassed, and for chemicals amply so. For steel capacity, and the output of cement, they were about reached.

In agriculture the target for aggregate production was reached, but some of the targets for relative adjustments in the outputs of different products were not. In its chapter on the "Results of the 3rd Plan," the 4th Plan reported that the output was almost as predicted for beef, but perceptibly below for veal, pork, and lamb. This account, from which it was concluded that "satisfactory progress" had been made towards the Plan's aim of changing the structure of agricultural production, and particularly of increasing the output of beef, was however based on the preliminary production figures. The corrected figures (as given by INSEE) showed a somewhat different picture. Even beef came below target and the increase in output since the agricultural "reference year" (1954) was only 22 percent instead of the 30 percent aimed at. On the whole, the attempt to solve the agricultural problem—which is France's major socioeconomic problem — has been unsuccessful, and we cannot say

that French "planning" was able to make much of a contribution. As we saw earlier, the 4th Plan took an almost hopeless view of this problem, and accepted increases in the surpluses of certain products as practically inevitable.

In the "non-basic" manufacturing sectors no "firm targets" had been established in the 3rd Plan but only "coherent forecasts compatible with the general expansion target." [5] The index of aggregate output for all of them taken together came somewhat below the forecast made by the Interim Plan. For individual industries there were of course wider deviations, plus or minus. The large sub-group "mechanical and electrical engineering" failed to reach the figure forecast (which had been kept unchanged as between the "initial" and the "Interim" Plans). The deviations become wider, of course, as we divide these broad sub-groups into narrower industry groups. The automobile industry, for example, for which the forecast had been raised in the "Interim Plan," came very far short of the new goal. The number of housing units completed (316,000 in 1961 compared with

---

[5] Cf. Text of the 4th Plan, p. 58.

274,000 in 1957) again exceeded the Plan's forecast (of 300,000) .

It was not possible to give, in the report on the execution of the 3rd Plan, a precise comparison between results and targets for investments by sector, owing to changes that had been made in the method of calculating the figures.

The 4th Plan (1962-65) appeared in the middle of its second year (1963) to be threatened, like its predecessor, with the need for a downward revision which the authorities were, however, doing their best to avoid. Productive investment was growing less fast than planned, and consumption faster, not only in the aggregate, but also per head. Moreover, inflation was once again a major problem; and in the autumn the government took new measures, following those already taken in the spring, to curb its advance. One sectoral target which looked as though it would require revision was that for steel,[6] the tendency towards too rapid an expansion of world capacity having caused French steel firms to make cuts in their investment programs. The overall growth rate, which in 1962 had been close to 7.0 percent

(and therefore well in excess of the 5.5 percent average envisaged by the Plan) , fell back in 1963 to about 4.5. In late 1963 and early 1964 the "stabilization plan" had for all practical purposes taken the place of "the Plan." And in the spring of 1964 it was officially conceded that the average target growth rate of the 4th Plan was not going to be reached. This was despite a bigger than predicted swelling of the employed labor force by "repatriates" from Algeria.

If we try to generalize from the experience of all the Plans, some of the chief points that emerge are the following:

1. Even the forecasts of the biggest aggregate, i.e., the increase in gross domestic output or the "growth rate" were not accurate enough to justify the degree of precision which the authorities had been seeking to give them as, for example, when they raised the target growth rate for the 4th Plan from 5.0 to 5.5 percent.

2. The record of the forecasts for the big sub-aggregates was, not very surprisingly, different from sector to sector and from Plan to Plan for one and the same sector. The

---

[6] See pp. 87-89 below for revision actually made.

record is best for the "basic" industries of the power sector that are nationalized. These forecasts were—except for coal—very good under the 3rd Plan, though less so under the previous ones. What happened under the 3rd Plan in the coal sector is a reflection of the well-known error which the French planners, like some international organizations, made in 1956-57 in foreseeing a general shortage of fuel in the near future, and in planning additional investments in the coal sector which very quickly turned out to be unnecessary and unprofitable. For the oil industry, too, the record is uneven. In other basic sectors (steel, aluminum, chemicals) the forecasts have in some instances been very wide of the mark. That this is true also for the basic agricultural products is perhaps a matter of course.

3. The divergences are normally much larger for the individual "non-basic" manufacturing industries than for the basic ones (except chemicals), though for the former group taken as a whole there is, naturally, a certain amount of canceling out between the positive and negative deviations for individual items.

4. It is not always true that sec-tor forecasts made for shorter periods are more accurate than those for longer ones. The Interim Plan, prepared much nearer to the terminal date of the 3rd Plan than the original Plan had been, made a poorer forecast for some branches, among them automobiles and some of the smaller manufacturing industries (outside the textiles and engineering groups).

5. The 2nd, 3rd, and 4th Plans all failed to give the promised approach to price stability. Between 1953 and 1957, the terminal year of the 2nd Plan, consumer prices rose by 5 percent and wholesale prices by 8 percent. Between 1957 and 1961, the terminal year of the 3rd Plan, there was a further increase of 30 percent in consumer prices and 22 percent in wholesale prices. Between 1961 and 1963, the second year of the 4th Plan, consumer prices rose by 10 percent and wholesale prices by 6 percent.

6. The 2nd, 3rd, and 4th Plans (though not the Interim Plan) all came very wide of the mark in their predictions of the development of exports and imports. This is in part due to the Plans' failure to predict the successive waves of domestic cost and price inflation. But French planners assume, even with-

out this factor, that the "uncontrolled foreign element" is an obstacle to accurate planning, and this is one reason why they wish to see French planning extended to a wider area, commencing with the other members of the European Common Market.

A point that merits special attention is the difficulty of accurately forecasting the future size and composition of the labor force, or even of knowing what the figures are at the present time, unless censuses are taken at very frequent intervals. Yet these are figures and forecasts on which all the production targets would seem inevitably to depend. They must surely be at least as important as the forecasts for the level of investments.

As remarked above, both the 3rd and the 4th Plans were made on the basis of the May 1954 Census of Population figures, and on estimates of what had happened or was going to happen after that. The 3rd Plan assumed that the total employed labor force available in 1961 would number 19,-250,000 persons (compared with 18,870,000 in 1954). This assumption was based, first, on the knowledge that there would only be a very small "natural" increase in

the labor force, supposing that the "activity rate" of the population remained constant. It relied, further, on a net new immigration of workers after 1954 of 360,000, on an increase in the proportion of women at work, leading to an estimated increase of 150,000 "active" persons; on a small decrease in the number of men "under the colors," and on a decrease of 80,000 in the numbers of unemployed. These four sources had, however, to make good a reduction of 250,000 due to the increase in the average duration of schooling.

There were here several elements of uncertainty. The immigration which actually took place was doubtless greater than estimated, though we have no exact figures, since only the foreign workers entering France are registered, and not those leaving. On the other hand, the number of the military in 1961, and at the height of the Algerian conflict, was very much higher than had been estimated (about 550,000 instead of 300,000). In addition the number of women at work, as the census of March 1962 showed, had not increased but slightly decreased. This census also revealed that very soon after the close of the 3rd Plan, the total employed labor force was 18,956,000,[7] or perceptibly lower than the figure assumed by the Plan.[8] It revealed other errors in the forecasts by big sectors of employment. The census figures, with those forecast by the Plan in brackets were as follows (in thousands) : agriculture 3,850 [9] (4,600); industry 7,324 (7,300); tertiary sector (including the "administrations" and the army) [10] 7,734 (7,350).

The 4th Plan did not, of course, have the 1962 census figures to consult. It remarked [11] that the actual employment level in 1961 was, according to the provisional estimates, lower (19,000,000) than forecast by the 3rd Plan, and that the latter had also underestimated the number of persons released from agriculture to other occupations. The 4th Plan proceeded to base its own predictions on the assumption that between 1954 and 1959 (the 4th Plan's "reference year"), the number of people employed in agriculture had fallen by 550,000, i.e., to 4,540,000, and it forecast that by 1965 the number would have declined further to about 4,100,000. The results of the Population Census taken in March 1962 showed, however, that by that date the agricultural labor force had already fallen to 3,850,000, or 250,000 below the figure assumed by the 4th Plan for 1965. In effect, the release of labor from agriculture assumed to take place during the 4th Plan had occurred before the Plan started.

Mention has been made of another factor which the Plan had been unable to predict, namely the number of people who would return to France from Algeria. About 700,000 actually came in, some 300,000 of them belonging to the labor force; and almost all of these have found employment. The number vastly exceeded that expected when the 4th Plan was drawn up. The Plan had allowed for an increase of 660,000 in the labor force, inclusive of "repatriates" and foreign immigrants, during the four years

---

[7] 100,000 of the addition shown by this figure compared with that (18,847,500) registered by the 1954 Census represents men serving in the regular army outside Metropolitan France and not counted in the 1954 Census, and hence is a purely accounting increase.
[8] Cf. preceding footnote.
[9] An additional 48,000 were engaged in fishing.
[10] Cf. footnote 7 above.
[11] Cf. Text of the 4th Plan, p. 53.

1962-65. It is officially estimated,[12] however, that during the *two* years 1962-63 the labor force increased by 800,000.

The planners might have expected—as some of them indeed did [13]—that if the forecasting in other directions were "good," this higher than predicted increase in the labor force would have caused the growth rate actually achieved to exceed that anticipated in the Plan. In fact the reverse seems to have occurred.[14]

---

[12] "Le Rapport économique et financier," *Statistique et Etudes financières,* November 1963, p. 1283.

[13] See pp. 79-80 below.

[14] In the national accounts presented with the Finance Bill for 1965, it was estimated that the growth rate actually achieved under the 4th Plan would be 5.3 percent instead of the "planned" 5.5 percent.

IX.

THE SIGNIFICANCE OF
THE PLAN'S FIGURES

The above examination of Plan figures raises a number of questions concerning their significance. First of all what is the value of the figures considered as a set of forecasts? What claims can be made for them as guides to the individual economic operator?

The Consistency Test and Better Coordination

The reader may be reminded (see pp. 18-19 above) of procedure. First the Vertical Commissions prepare the forecasts (corresponding to the overall growth rate and other general objectives of the Plan) of production, exports, imports, investments, manpower requirements, etc., for their individual branches and sub-branches. Then all the forecasts are put together, and tested for consistency with each other and with the general aims of the Plan. Inconsistencies are reported back to the Commissions by the Commissariat which, at the same time, indicates the "arbitrages" it proposes for overcoming them.

The 4th Plan describes this process with special reference to the non-basic manufacturing industries, which, it says, present the most difficult problem in this connection, because of their diversity and dissimilar rates of expansion, and in some cases (e.g., that of the clothing industry) still inadequate statistics. The description is as follows:

> However great the care taken in the work of synthesizing the forecasts, it is not possible to guarantee perfect consistency, between for example the forecasts of the purchases of a product by a customer-branch and the forecasts of the sales of that same product by the supplying branch. But each time a serious distortion appeared, consistency was reestablished by agreement between the branches concerned. Similarly the work of synthesizing the Plan led quite often to a modification of the foreign trade forecasts, each branch having, very legitimately, the tendency to fix high export targets for itself, and to foresee low imports. In some cases this led us to draw a distinction between the target inserted in the Plan, and consistent with the general equilibrium forecasts for foreign trade, and the more ambitious target fixed for itself by the branch. It is, of course, the first which figures in the tables (of the Plan). In the other cases, the new target was fixed in agreement with the representatives of the branch. . . . [1]

In some cases, then, sectors or sub-sectors had been persuaded to revise their figures for output, exports, etc., upwards or downwards; and in other cases, the Commissariat had made revisions on its own responsibility.

---

[1] Cf. Text of 4th Plan, p. 361.

Now both in the texts of the Plans, and in the literature about them, a great deal of emphasis has been placed on the advantages of establishing a system of "targets of production and foreign trade which are consistent with each other and with the overall targets" [2] of the Plan. It is said, for instance, that the "psychological factor," mentioned earlier,[3] is reinforced by the "logical element" which resides in the proven internal consistency of the Plan, and which makes it seem reasonable to conform to its forecasts.[4] As Mr. Massé puts it,[5] "The Plan plays the part of a 'generalized market'. . . . Every branch of activity is promised the possibility of acquiring its productive factors and selling its goods on a balanced market." He adds, however, an important qualification: "The promise is . . . only kept if everybody plays the game"; and it "merely acts as an incentive. It is not binding on anybody."

This "coordinating action" of the Plan is held to be partly responsible for the greater efficiency of investment [6] in France since the war, compared with other countries. Some foreign commentators, as, for example, Professor James Tobin in the United States, share the view that French planning has worked in this way.[7]

There is a question, however, as to the practical importance of the proven internal consistency of the set of forecasts embodied in the Plan. Obviously the consistency test would have worked with numerous sets of hypothetical data alternative to the set chosen, including the set which actual events showed to be the "right" one. The fact that the particular set—not necessarily the "right" one—contained in the Plan passes this test is not itself a proof that the individual plans of firms are thereby better coordinated in any effective sense. The individual operators, though they may be influenced by the Plan's forecasts, do not strictly follow them. They can, and do, proceed as current market developments, and their own esti-

---

[2] *Ibid.*
[3] Pp. 61-62.
[4] Cf. La Documentation française illustrée, 4ème Plan, p. 139.
[5] French Methods of Planning," *op. cit.*
[6] Cf., for example, Wickham, *op. cit.*, p. 345, and the OECD Report mentioned above.
[7] Cf. his article "How Planned is Our Economy?" *New York Times Magazine,* October 13, 1963, p. 113.

mates of what is going to happen in the future, indicate they should; and they adjust their own private plans continually during the four years covered by the official Plan. Again in the words of Mr. Massé:

Firms are not dispensed (by the existence of the Plan) from working out their valuations and choosing their own attitude concerning risk. But they do so in a better-informed manner. . . . Partial adjustments remain necessary while the plan is being carried out, under the influence of the market, operating in a frame which allows it to work more smoothly. Thus the economy retains its flexibility and every participant a feeling of liberty.[8]

But what, then, has happened to the influence of the Plan as a consistent set of forecasts which hold together only if everybody "plays the game"? Has it disintegrated and been replaced by the spontaneous forces of the market? "Playing the game" would seem to be compatible with "making the necessary partial adjustments" only when the forecasting is of a high degree of accuracy, and the necessary adjustments, therefore, only

very small. When this is not the case, the "flexibility" of the Plan would appear to destroy its "coordinating function."

This point may be illustrated by events that happened early in the span of the 4th Plan. In June 1962, when almost half of the first year of the Plan was already over, the question was raised, in the Investment Section of the Economic and Social Council, as to whether it would be possible and advisable in view of the unexpectedly large number of repatriates coming in from Algeria, and of the reduction in the length of military service, to "adopt" a higher average annual rate of growth for the three last years of the Plan (1963-65) than that originally set (i.e., to take 6.0 instead of 5.5 percent). The Council's Section was in favor of doing this, Mr. Massé hesitant. The higher rate was not in fact "adopted." But if it had been, it would have at once invalidated both of the sets of detailed sectoral forecasts that had been laboriously made by the Commissions (first for a 5.0, and then for a 5.5 percent growth rate), and have rendered irrelevant the consistency tests which these forecasts

---

[8] Cf. article cited in footnote 5 above.

had passed. Alternatively, the Commissions would have had to be recalled to do the same work all over again for the third time. In fact, with or without a change in the "adopted" growth rate, it was the market which was doing the coordinating of economic activities; and, in 1962 and 1963, it was coordinating them into a pattern (determined by the actual development of domestic consumption, foreign trade, etc.) which was perceptibly different, in some very important respects, from what the Plan had forecast. The pattern which the planners had successfully submitted to the consistency test never had more than a fictitious existence.

So long, then, as the Plan does not succeed in achieving a high degree of accuracy in its forecasting, for each and all of the sectors, the question remains as to whether it means anything to say that economic developments have been "coordinated" or "guided" by the Plan.

Another question that poses itself is: Does the Plan's forecasting procedure serve only to augment the operators' chances of hitting the bull's eye, or can it also diminish them? The answer sometimes

given by planners is that the effect can only be in the right direction and never in the wrong. They argue that the Plan's forecasts essentially reproduce those made by the operators themselves (through the Commissions), and cannot therefore be said to lead, or mislead, them into following predictions less valid than those they would have made independently of the Plan. Thanks to the planning procedure, it is said, these forecasts are made in a better-informed manner. This answer is not fully convincing for at least three reasons.

First, the operators' own forecasts are, or may be, influenced by the rates for overall growth, and for the growth in aggregate investment and consumption respectively, "suggested" to them by the planning authorities as an "indicative" framework for their individual branch and sub-branch forecasts. Thus, when the growth rate for productive investment was set too high by the authorities as under the 4th Plan, it may have been a factor leading to overexpansion of certain equipment-goods branches on a scale greater than would have occurred had the firms been guided by their own independent estimates of growth rates. *Secondly,* the operators are in some instances persuaded by the Commissariat to revise the forecasts (made to fit into the "indicative" framework) for their individual branches and sub-branches. *Thirdly,* it is likely that the more authority there is behind a forecast, the more confidence will some at least of the operators be inclined to place in it.

We cannot, therefore, be sure that either individual firms, or whole branches, or the economy as a whole, made better rather than worse forecasts as the result of the planning procedure.

An Illustration

Some of the points discussed above may be exemplified by reference to recent happenings in two industries, automobiles and steel.

The French automobile industry is now sufficiently important for errors of under- or overestimation of its market possibilities, and of its need for expanding capacity, to have serious consequences for the French economy as a whole. In 1962 the output, in terms of the number of cars (passenger plus commercial) produced, was three times what it had been ten years

earlier; and by 1961-62 it was nearly equal to Britain's output, though inferior to that of West Germany.

The "results" of the 3rd Plan showed the industry (here defined to include motorcycles and cycles) as having fallen short in 1961 of the target level set by the original Plan, and *very much* short of the revised level set by the Interim Plan. The 1961 output figures on the base 1956=100 were as follows: forecast made by 3rd Plan 146; forecast by Interim Plan 165; level actually reached only 133. But, as already remarked, the terminal year of the 3rd Plan (1961) happened to be one of especially low output for the automobile industry. The production index (again on the base 1956=100) for the pre-terminal year (1960) had been 144, and therefore not far short of the "target" of the original 3rd Plan, though still very much below that of the Interim Plan.

The 4th Plan put the target for this industry in 1965 at 1.7 million cars [9] compared with an actual output of less than 1.2 million in 1961 (and 1.3 million in 1960). The producers had originally suggested a

---

[9] Included are private cars plus commercial vehicles of less than a certain weight (4 metric tons).

somewhat higher 1965 target, namely 1.85 million, but the Commissariat had persuaded them that this figure should be reduced, on the grounds that it corresponded to export estimates which "a concern for prudence" advised cutting.[10] Late in 1963, however, it appeared that by the end of that year the target for 1965 (the terminal year of the Plan) would almost have been reached. In two years the industry's output had grown by as much (40 percent) as it ought, according to the Plan, to have grown in four. It' was the domestic demand for cars that had grown faster than foreseen; and imports as well as domestic production had followed suit. Thus the number of cars (domestic and imported) bought by Frenchmen in 1963 (1.26 million) was already in excess of the number forecast for 1965 (1.12 million).[11] Foreign demand, and therefore exports, had not progressed faster than predicted by the Plan. In this instance, therefore, it was not the peculiar difficulty of predicting develop-

ments abroad,[12] as opposed to those at home, that had been the cause of the planners' "miscalculations." [13]

Roughly the reverse of the situation in the automobile industry had at the same time (1962-63) occurred in the steel industry. Under the 3rd Plan, as we saw, this industry had almost exactly reached the target, which had been kept unchanged as between the original 3rd Plan, and the Interim Plan. The 4th Plan had expressed itself in very optimistic terms about the expanding market prospects for the French steel industry. It put the 1965 target capacity at 24.5 million tons per year (representing an increase of 33 percent over the 1961 level), and estimated that actual output in 1965 would be between 22 and 24 million tons. But French crude steel output, which had risen uninterruptedly from 1,120 thousand metric tons per month in 1956 to 1,268 in 1959, and 1,467 in 1961, actually fell back a little (to 1,436 thousand) in 1962,[14] instead of increasing further; and in 1963 the

---

[10] Text of the 4th Plan, p. 374.

[11] Information provided by Mr. Massé in the communication mentioned below.

[12] See p. 74 above concerning emphasis placed by planners on this point.

[13] 1964 was, however, a year of stagnation for the automobile industry, and it is possible that output in 1965 may not be much higher than forecast by the Plan.

[14] OECD figures.

industry succeeded only in just about restoring the 1961 position.

Thus, in the first two years of the 4th Plan this industry had made no progress at all towards achieving the roughly 30 percent increase in output that it was supposed to achieve in four. France's experience in this sector was running parallel to that of the two other big Western European producers, West Germany (the largest) and Britain. As was mentioned above, the limitation on expansion was here coming largely from the increased competition on world markets of new steel countries.

Thus, half way through the 4th Plan, it appeared that at least two important industries were failing to keep to the Plan. And a good part of the equipment-goods sector was also behind schedule, as was to be expected seeing that the predicted growth rate for productive investment was not being reached.

The Dilemma of "Soft" Planning: What is "Planned"?

These events—as others before them—were bound to give rise to queries as to what the Plan really meant, or whether it was a "plan"

at all. To some members of the public its meaning was increasingly puzzling, as may be judged from the following incident. Late in December 1963, Mr. Alain Rambaud, in a letter to *Le Monde,* expressed his bewilderment in face of what had recently happened in the automobile industry. Admitting, he said, that "the execution of the Plan cannot always exactly fit the forecasts, and that adjustments may be necessary during the course of its execution," still the fact that an industry increased its rate of growth so far beyond that indicated by the Plan as the automobile industry had done must raise serious questions. The industry had, by pressing on the labor market, and on the supplies of various products and services, contributed to the inflationary tendencies, which the government had been obliged to combat by its stabilization policy (launched in September and reinforced in November). Was it right that "certain industrialists (and among them a nationalized enterprise) "[15] should "consider the Plan as just a scrap of paper and refuse to follow, even approximately, its directives? Either the Plan is use-

---

[15] The Renault Motor Works.

less," he continued, "and then it is a piece of hypocrisy to consider it as an 'ardent obligation' [as the Head of State had done] and to surround it with so much verbal devotion: or else it constitutes a rule of national life, and everybody must undertake to follow its directives, it then being the role of the government to give support to those who are unable to keep up, and to hold back those who bolt ahead."

Mr. Massé replied to this letter. He explained that the reason why the domestic demand for cars had risen so much more rapidly than forecast by the Plan was partly that aggregate consumption had grown faster than planned, but partly, also, that the proportions between consumers' expenditures on different items had not been as forecast; and he remarked that the Plan had explicitly pointed out that these proportions must be assumed flexible.[16] He agreed, however, that Mr. Rambaud's letter had a real point, which was that "the distinction between what is, in the Plan, a target and what a forecast, has not yet been sufficiently well clarified." It was a point, he said, which

would merit a lot of attention in the 5th Plan.

The Difficulty of Distinguishing Targets from Forecasts

We do not yet know just where the 5th Plan is going to draw the line. The task of working out a valid distinction looks like being a difficult one. Conceptually, various possibilities suggest themselves. In practice, all of them present problems.

1. Should we accept the division tentatively suggested in the 4th Plan between "non-basic manufacturing industries" and "basic industries" (defined in the 4th Plan as those in the fuel and power sector, steel, aluminum, chemicals, and cement)? As already remarked, it has sometimes proved just as difficult to make accurate forecasts for steel, coal, and chemicals as for the non-basic industries. But should the basic industries nonetheless have "firm targets" assigned to them? And would it then be proper to hold such an industry back if it threatened to "bolt ahead" (as chemicals, for instance, had bolted in the past), and to help it forward if it were falling

---

[16] See p. 29 above.

behind (as steel was doing in 1962-63)? Or should (and could) only the lame horses be helped forward without the bolters being restrained?

2. Should the Plan be considered as a "real" Plan only for the public sector, including the nationalized industries? Some of the planners have argued that even as matters stand the Plan, while being "indicative" for the private sector, is "imperative" for the public sector. As regards the present situation, this distinction lacks substance, however. For even in the public sector, deviations from the Plan do, and are bound to, occur. This is true not merely of the nationalized industries but also of the "traditional" public activities. Even with the Plan, and in the comparatively serene years since the financial rehabilitation of 1958-59, the French Government has not managed to get along with only one budget annually. In each year, up to and including 1963, it presented two or three supplementaries.

3. Should the Plan go still higher in the hierarchy from subaggregates to aggregates, i.e., to the overall growth rate, and consider only this, along perhaps with the investment and consumption growth rates, as

genuine targets? Even this solution has its difficulties. The "instrumentation" of the Plan (as distinguished from its alleged coordinating function) is at present primarily geared to investments made by some, not all, individual firms, rather than to aggregate saving or investment, and through this the growth rate. The latter are influenced only by the sum of the influences on the former, and by the "classical" instruments of monetary and fiscal policy. But this part of economic policy is something which the successive Plans have, up till now, left totally "unplanned." The 4th Plan, for example, had proposed a certain increase in the rate of investment without explaining how this was to be achieved. Similarly, it proposed a specific increase in the growth rate, but gave no clear indication as to how this could be accomplished.

It is in any event difficult to see how, under "soft" planning, an exact future growth rate can—in the terminology now current in France—be "planned," "chosen," "adopted," or "fixed" by the authorities, unless these words are to lose their meaning. This is so not merely because the authorities are powerless to control certain determinants of the rate (such as technical progress and other innovations, or the weather, or developments abroad), but also because, under "soft" planning, they deliberately refrain from planning others (such as the way in which the public distributes income between consumption and savings).

4. A final possibility is to say that the only real objectives of the Plan are certain general aims of economic policy expressed in qualitative terms (e.g., achieving a high rate of economic growth, with full employment, and in conditions of price stability and balance-of-payments equilibrium; improving the relative income position of the poorer classes; industrializing underdeveloped regions; and so on), and to abandon the practice of setting targets in precise quantitative terms, even if very rough statistical magnitudes, recognized as being indeterminate between more or less wide limits, are attached to them.

If this last course is chosen, it seems to mean that our search for a way of sifting the real targets from the mere forecasts has left us only with forecasts.

The Quest for Greater Forecasting Accuracy

The difficulty of making a valid distinction between targets and forecasts would solve itself if all the Plan's forecasts were accurate, or very nearly so, since the distinction between the two things would then disappear. And it is in this direction, of more "efficient" forecasting, that many people look for an ultimate solution of the present dilemma of "soft" planning.

Two ways of achieving this improvement are envisaged. One view is that the solution lies in the adoption of "short-term" planning within the "medium-term" plan. Those who hold this view remind us once again that one of the advantages of French planning is the "flexibility" that goes with its "softness." What matters they say is not whether the figures are right to start with, but only that they should be "revised in time." Steps have been taken with this intention. Since 1959, the Finance Bill, when presented to Parliament in the autumn, has included an annual "economic budget" consisting of forecasts for the coming year of the movements in the main aggregates (national product, gross investment, consumption, industrial output, imports, exports, the price level), and also of developments in some of the principal branches of industry. The view is widely held that it should be the normal practice to make a more thorough overall revision of the Plan (in the manner followed in the Interim Plan of 1960) whenever a very sharp divergence of events from the originally predicted course makes this seem desirable.

A proposal for thus revising the 4th Plan was considered in 1963. The Commissariat consulted the Modernization Commissions concerning the advisability of revising certain of their targets for 1965.[17] The Steel Commission proposed a reduction of 2 million tons in the industry's capacity target. Other Commissions indicated that the production targets in some branches or sub-branches might not be reached, while in some they might be exceeded. The Commissariat concluded, however, that only the steel and housing targets needed to be "formally" adjusted,[18] and that

there was no necessity for proceeding to a general revision of the Plan or of its "fundamental objectives." Only one of these, it said, seemed to be definitely in need of revision, and that was the foreign trade balance: imports would be higher, and exports lower than originally forecast—but this need not affect the other objectives of the Plan! By the spring of 1964, it had become more obvious that the "fundamental objectives" might not be reached. But it was not suggested that a revised Interim Plan should be drawn up. The Commissariat was by this time very fully occupied with the preparation of the 5th Plan.

Some of the planners themselves regard the solution of periodic revisions as being, even in principle, unsatisfactory. It is likely, as Professor Bauchet has said,[19] to make the Plan more annual than pluriannual, and it would thus take away an essential part of the Plan's "Frenchness," namely its medium-term character, by virtue of which it differs from the short-term (an-

---

[17] Cf. *Rapport sur l'Exécution du Plan en 1962 et 1963, op. cit.,* pp. 37 ff.

[18] Later in the year the petroleum industry (*Comité professionel du pétrole*) published revised 1965 targets for its branch. The figure for refining capacity was raised from 54 to 63 million metric tons (i.e., by 16 percent), and the figure for the amount of crude oil to be processed from 45.5 to 53.4 million tons.

[19] *Op. cit.,* pp. 177-78.

nual) planning carried out by, for example, the Netherlands. And the more the period for which the Plan is supposed to be *effectively* valid is shortened the greater the doubt as to whether the Plan is really guiding economic development, or whether it is merely registering that development after the event.

Practical problems add to these difficulties of principle. The adoption of any proposal for continuous revision of the Plan would almost inevitably deprive "French" planning of a second of its most characteristic traits, namely the special method (involving the machinery of the Commissions) by which the Plan is prepared. For this method could scarcely be used at annual intervals. It would thus be impossible to revise all the detailed figures by branch and sub-branch, and the Plan would in effect come to consist only of forecasts of the big aggregates and a few of the larger subaggregates. In these conditions it would become increasingly apparent that the detailed work done by the Commissions in the preparing of the original Plan was of doubtful utility. We should notice, for instance, that the revision of

targets made in a few big industries in 1963, and mentioned above, were really only public announcements—useful enough in their own way we may say—of these industries' new prospects. There was no question of fitting them into a "coherent" system that passed the "consistency test."

The second expectation of improvement anticipates that the accuracy of medium-term forecasting will increase as time goes on, and as the techniques of forecasting improve. Mr. Wickham, in the article [20] quoted earlier, thought he could already see, in the case of France, signs of a progressive reduction in the deviations of the results of the Plans from their targets. But he was speaking only of the "global targets" or big aggregates (national product, industrial output, agricultural output, private consumption, investment), and even for these the evidence is now thinner than it seemed when he wrote.

As regards the subaggregates, or the quantities that are of direct importance for individual business sectors and firms, it seems doubtful whether the forecasting can be-

---

[20] P. 346.

come highly accurate in this age of rapid technological change, and in an advanced society where successful entrepreneurship is often bound up with the launching of new products and the developing of new tastes. An official description [21] of France's 4th Plan speaks of the need for a "sort of passion for innovation" as a part of "export strategy." And it would seem to be quite generally true that one of the conditions for national economic success in the modern world is that industry should be flexible and easily adaptable to changing events, not tied to immutable "targets." This is quite apart from political hazards. The war in Indo-China, the war in Algeria, the domestic political crisis of 1958, the question of whether Great Britain would or would not enter the European Economic Community, the way in which military expenditures might develop in connection with the *force de frappe* were all important events or prospects which the Plan either deliberately did not, or in some cases could not, take into account. They belonged, or were treated as belonging, to the vast realm of unpredictable contingencies.

---

[21] La Documentation française illustrée, 4ème Plan, p. 27.

X.

ON THE EVE OF THE FIFTH PLAN

In the spring of 1964 it was officially recommended, by the National Accounts Commission, that the main targets (for 1965) of the 4th Plan should be abandoned. The lag of actual performance behind the target rates up to that time was seemingly too great for the economy to catch up unless internal and external financial equilibrium were to be sacrificed. The 4th Plan had, to all intents and purposes, been replaced by the "stabilization plan," aimed at curbing inflation, and saving France from a repetition of the financial crisis of 1958 and from a new devaluation of the franc. The 4th Plan had in effect suffered the same fate as the 3rd.

Recognizing the failure of two successive Plans did not mean— not as yet at least—that the very existence of the Plan was being officially called into question. The National Accounts Commission itself took the line that the most important thing was not that output should catch up by 1965 with the target level set by the 4th Plan, but that the 5th Plan should start off on the right foot, and should go forward in conditions that gave it good chances of success. Mr. Massé is reported to have remarked that, after all, the fundamental aim of the 4th Plan was "expansion with stability," a description which seemed to make the whole elaborate structure of the Plan, and its costly method of preparation, look superfluous. For some time before this, however, increasingly insistent voices had been asking whether France really had a Plan, and had been pointing to the contradictions of a policy which swayed uncertainly between the "ardent obligation of the Plan" on the one side, and the restoration of a "liberal economy" governed by market mechanisms on the other. The London *Economist*, in its issue of May 23, 1964, carried an article entitled "French Planning De-

mondée." It was too early, however, to conclude that planning was going out of fashion in France, or even that its partisans were fewer than before. At a conference of French language economists held in Paris in the last week of May two papers about French planning were discussed, one by a non-planner, Professor Daniel Villey, and another by a planner, Professor Bauchet. Only one speaker, Professor Maurice Alais, out of some 20, sided with the first.

Nonetheless it is true that, not so long after French planning had been taken up with enthusiasm in Britain and in other countries, it was beginning to be regarded in France as very ambiguous—neither fish nor fowl. This ambiguousness was placing a growing strain on the credulity of the public, and the *mystique* of the Plan was beginning to lose its hold.

At the same time a new current of opinion—or perhaps we should say an old one revived—had been asserting itself. Since early 1962 there had been signs, particularly among the younger generation of leftist intellectuals, but not only there, of an increasing disaffection for purely "indicative" or "soft" planning. There were demands for making the Plan harder and more effective. This would imply two things:

(a) making the Plan specify clearly which are the targets, general and sectoral, that it definitely aims at reaching, and sharply distinguishing these from mere forecasts;

(b) sharpening the instruments for enforcing compliance, and perhaps also increasing their number.

There is a variety of views as to what the instrumentation should be. One view is that the Plan should be implemented through the practically complete control over the allocation of the means of finance (capital issues and lending by the long-term credit institutes and the banks), some going even so far as to demand the control of financing from retained earnings. Another view favors the retention of the eclectic method, using a large number of instruments, including the present ones (control over the use of funds, fiscal incentives, subsidies, etc), but perhaps with others added. As possible additions have been suggested:

1. Control over the allocation of industrial and commercial building permits, along the lines already followed in the Paris area, for the whole of France.

2. Imposition of penalties for non-compliance with the Plan's objectives, one such penalty being nationalization.

3. Making the Plan operate, in chosen sectors at least, at the level of the firm.

4. Setting up of State enterprises in sectors or localities where private enterprise is "not doing its job" as this is conceived by the Plan.

5. Incorporation in the Plan of an incomes policy.

Meanwhile the preparation of the 5th Plan, started in 1962, had been going ahead. The new Plan will contain a number of novelties with respect to its predecessors. Its method of preparation is more complicated, and its contents will be more complex. Its "democratization," as already noted, requires the presentation to Parliament of a number of variants concerning the "fundamental options." It will run for five years instead of four. It is going to be more highly "regionalized" than was the preceding Plan, and in this connection consultations are to take place with newly formed local economic development commissions in the 21 "program regions." It will also contain an incomes policy, presumably only "indicative" in character. The definite targets will be more clearly distinguished from what are merely "forecasts," "desirable developments," or "recommendations." The growth rate will presumably remain a target, but it is possible that the figure, besides being set this time on the cautious side, will be considered flexible within certain limits. Indeed "flexibility" (*souplesse*) is, according to Mr. Pompidou, going to be more than ever the keynote of French planning in the future. For the 5th Plan must, he says, "draw the lessons of the 4th."

French attitudes towards French planning at the present time may be summarized by distinguishing three main groups. One is that led by Mr. Massé, who continues to insist on the softness and flexibility of the Plan, and to present it as the ally and not the enemy of the

market economy. This conception of the Plan has recently received the open support of Mr. Pompidou, and is doubtless shared by other important members of the present government. To the right is a quiet, and probably relatively small, but nonetheless influential group, whose aim is simply to complete the process of restoring a market economy in France, and who regard the whole notion of "French planning" with skepticism even if they do not all openly attack it. The main spokesman of this group is Mr. Jacques Rueff. On the left is a large and vocal group, or perhaps we should say plurality of groups, whose views do not coincide on all points, but who are agreed in thinking that "indicative" planning should give way to planning of a more solid kind —the "real thing." Their proposals as to the extent and forms of State intervention in the economy which this would imply are many and various.

XI.

CONCLUSIONS

1. It is impossible to say how great an influence French economic planning has had on French postwar economic growth, or even whether it has on balance helped or hindered growth. We have no means of measuring the relative weight of various features in terms of their effect on productivity or total output. On one side of the ledger, for example, may be put the beneficial effects of (a) the regroupings into the larger units achieved in certain industries as the result of "persuasion" exerted through the government-business consulting machinery of the Plan, and (b) the general "informing" or "guiding" action of the Plan. But were these sufficient to offset

the harmful effects of (c) the weakening of competition to which the planning machinery may perhaps have led in some industries, and (d) the withholding of investment funds from the most profitable uses in favor of less profitable ones which must sometimes have occurred as a consequence of the capital-issues and credit controls and of the various selective investment "incentives."

Those people who claim to know with certainty that the total effect of French planning on economic growth was positive, and who may estimate that it was responsible for as much as, say, 1 percent of the average of roughly 5 percent over the last decade or more, are relying on an intuitive judgment. So would be those, if there were any, who pretended to know that the effect was negative; although in their case the judgment would perhaps, more often than not, be called "prejudice" against any form of economic planning. It is nonetheless possible to encounter, in French circles that are above suspicion on this score, the same view that we are at a loss to know whether the sum of all the effects of French planning on growth has so far been positive or negative.

There is room here for a neutral position, to which those "prejudiced" in favor of economic planning (though not necessarily "French planning"), and those "prejudiced" against, may alike adhere. It is that the net effect either way has been small. The puzzle as to which position is correct remains.

2. It is possible that "unplanned" inflation—leading to periodic financial crises, and to distortions in the price structure of which many still remain—may have had more influence on the course of French economic development than French planning. It has, however, long been argued by certain economists, and seems now to be officially regarded as a lesson of the 4th Plan, that the one thing may lead to the other. If the Plan commits the government to a policy of trying to reach investment and overall growth rates higher than the level of savings will support, it will tend to produce reluctance on the part of the authorities to take the necessary anti-inflationary measures in time. In one case, that of the 2nd Plan, this argument did not apply, since the inflation was on that occasion brought about by exceeding the

planned growth rate instead of keeping to it. On the whole, however, France's experience shows how a rigid growth rate policy, with the growth rate set—as many planners have in the past at least thought it should be—"on the high side," conflicts with the maintenance of financial stability. This was very clear in France by 1963-64.

3. By this time, too, it was becoming increasingly evident to the thinking public that the Plan, with its elaborate method of preparation, and its vast array of targets or forecasts, presented an impressive façade with little behind. The twin virtues of "softness" and "flexibility," which so strongly recommended France's particular brand of planning to other Western countries, had by now made its very existence seem doubtful in France. Either it was soon going to appear to a large part of the general public as bluff, or the accepted meaning of the term "Plan," or "planned economy," would have to be very different from the traditional one which still governed most of the thinking on the subject. There was evident need for official clarification on this point. One tendency now observable is, in fact, to abandon the notion of

the "Plan" as a set of precise aims which the planning authorities have the intention and the power to implement, and to regard it instead as only a set of detailed medium-term forecasts or, in Mr. Massé's words, as a "general market survey."

4. In view especially of the fate of the last two Plans, both of them more or less "abandoned" in midstream, even the importance of the Plan as a detailed overall forecasting service might be called into doubt. It does not appear, for example, that the Plan has so far helped individual industries (such as steel or automobiles) to assess their development prospects in a "better-informed manner" than the same industries were able to do in countries with no central forecasting service of the French kind. It remains the conviction of most French planners, however, that the forecasts are worth making in the way and in the detail that they are made. There is confidence that the forecasting, which is as they say still only in the experimental stage, will become more accurate in the future, especially if "French planning" is extended to the whole of the European Common Market taken as a unit. Some planners,

however, also see the need for stronger action towards *imposing* the Plan's targets in certain important sectors, at least, as a condition for achieving the more effective "coordination" or "guidance" of economic activity by the Plan.

5. The increased complexity which, in a formal sense at least, is going to characterize the 5th Plan with respect to its predecessors (its "regionalization," for example) has already caused some industrialists to fear as a consequence increased pressure toward more rigorous methods of implementing the Plan, and to suspect that in this way so-called "soft" or "indicative" planning may develop into "hard" or "imperative" planning. This does not at the moment appear to be the intention of the present government. Other circles in France are, however, pressing for a movement in this direction.

6. On the eve of the 5th Plan, then, a big question mark existed concerning what French planning was likely to become in the future. Would it, for a while at least, come to consist, either explicitly or implicitly, of mere forecasting? Or would it, over the longer run, develop into something much less

original than "French planning" is supposed to be, and much more similar to the kind of economic regimentation which Western countries associate with "Eastern planning"?

7. I have expressed doubts, such as are shared by many planners in France, as to whether French planning in its present form can truly be regarded as "central planning of the economy." This is, of course, not equivalent to denying that France has been, and is, making progress toward greater rationality and coherence in some fields at least of her general economic policy, or that certain highly desirable structural changes in her industry have resulted from the government-business consultations that form part of her planning machinery. These features are, however, dissociable from "central planning of the economy" in the strict sense, and should preferably be kept conceptually and terminologically distinct. France could and would continue to foster the one practice even if she gave up the other. What remained might, it is true, still rank as "central economic planning" in the broad sense in which this term is currently used in some other Western

countries. But again it would be something different from "French planning" as it was originally conceived and still is regarded by many of its advocates as well as by the public at large in France.

I have not tried to predict in which of the two possible directions—right or left—French planning will actually move in the future if its present unstable position becomes untenable.

SHORT BIBLIOGRAPHY

Official publications:

Conseil National du Crédit, Rapports annuels.

Ministère des Finances, Statistiques et Etudes Financières.

IVe Plan de Développement économique et social (1962-65), 1962.

La Documentation française illustrée, 4ème Plan, October-November 1962.

Books, pamphlets, and articles:

Bauchet, P., *La Planification française,* 1962. (English translation available, London, 1964)

Bauchard, P., *La Mystique du Plan,* 1963.

Bloch-Lainé, F., *A la Recherche d'une Economie Concertée,* 1959.

Bloch-Lainé, *Pour une Réforme de l'Entreprise,* 1963.

Cazes, B., *La Planification en France et le 4ème Plan,* 1962.

Fourastié, J. and Courthéoux, J.-P., *La Planification économique en France,* 1963.

Gascuel, A., *Aspects du 4ème Plan,* 1962.

Hackett, J. and A.-M., *Economic Planning in France,* 1963.

de Jouvenel, B., "Planning in France—Techniques and Lessons," *Moorgate and Wall Street,* Autumn 1961.

PEP, *Economic Planning in France,* August 1961.

PEP, *French Planning: Some Lessons for Britain,* September 1963.

Perroux, E., *Le quatrième Plan français,* 1962.

Sheahan, J., *Promotion and Control of Industry in Post-War France,* 1963.

Villey, D., "Marché et Plan," *Revue d'Economie Politique,* 1964.

Wickham, S., "French Planning: Retrospect and Prospect," *The Review of Economics and Statistics,* November 1963.

For other references, see the bibliographies given by P. Bauchet and by J. and A.-M. Hackett.

PUBLICATIONS

STUDIES

The Free Society, *Clare E. Grffiin*— 1965, 138 pp. ($4.50)

Congress and the Federal Budget, *Murray L. Weidenbaum* and *John S. Saloma III*—1965, 209 pp. ($4.00)

Poverty: Definition and Perspective, *Rose D. Friedman*—1965

The Responsible Use of Power: A Critical Analysis of the Congressional Budget Process, *John S. Saloma III*— 1964

Federal Budgeting—The Choice of Government Programs, *Murray L. Weidenbaum*—1964

The Rural Electrification Administration —An Evaluation, *John D. Garwood* and *W. C. Tuthill*—1963

The Economic Analysis of Labor Union Power, Revised Edition, *Edward H. Chamberlin*—1963

United States Aid to Yugoslavia and Poland — Analysis of a Controversy, *Milorad M. Drachkovitch*—1963

Communists in Coalition Governments, *Gerhart Niemeyer*—1963

Subsidized Food Consumption, *Don Paarlberg*—1963

Automation—The Impact of Technological Change, *Yale Brozen*—1963

Essay on Apportionment and Representative Government, *Alfred de Grazia* —1963 ($2.00)

American Foreign Aid Doctrines, *Edward C. Banfield*—1963

The Rescue of the Dollar, *Wilson E. Schmidt*—1963

The Role of Gold, *Arthur Kemp*—1963

Pricing Power and "Administrative" Inflation—Concepts, Facts and Policy Implications, *Henry W. Briefs*—1962

Depreciation Reform and Capital Replacement, *William T. Hogan*—1962

The Federal Antitrust Laws, *Jerrold G. Van Cise*—1962

Consolidated Grants: A Means of Maintaining Fiscal Responsibility, *George C. S. Benson* and *Harold F. McClelland*— 1961

Inflation: Its Causes and Cures, Revised and Enlarged Edition, *Gottfried Haberler*—1961

The Patchwork History of Foreign Aid, *Lorna Morley and Felix Morley*—1961

U. S. Immigration Policy and World Population Problems, *Virgil Salera*— 1960

Voluntary Health Insurance in the United States, *Rita R. Campbell* and *W. Glenn Campbell*—1960

Unionism Reappraised: From Classical Unionism to Union Establishment, *Goetz Briefs*—1960

United States Aid and Indian Economic Development, *P. T. Bauer*—1959

Improving National Transportation Policy, *John H. Frederick*—1959

The Question of Governmental Oil Import Restrictions. *William H. Peterson*— 1959

Labor Unions and the Concept of Public Service, *Roscoe Pound*—1959

Labor Unions and Public Policy, *Edward H. Chamberlin, Philip D. Bradley, Gerard D. Reilly,* and *Roscoe Pound*— 1958, 177 pp. ($2.00)

National Aid to Higher Education, *George C. S. Benson* and *John M. Payne* —1958

Agricultural Surpluses and Export Policy, *Raymond F. Mikesell*—1958

Post-War West German and United Kingdom Recovery, *David McCord Wright*—1957

The Regulation of Natural Gas, *James W. McKie*—1957

Legal Immunities of Labor Unions, *Roscoe Pound*—1957

*Automation—Its Impact on Economic Growth and Stability, *Almarin Phillips* —1957

*Involuntary Participation in Unionism, *Philip D. Bradley*—1956

The Role of Government in Developing Peaceful Uses of Atomic Energy, *Arthur Kemp*—1956

The Role of The Federal Government in Housing, *Paul F. Wendt*—1956

The Upper Colorado Reclamation Project, Pro by *Sen. Arthur V. Watkins,* Con by *Raymond Moley*—1956

*Federal Aid to Education—Boon or Bane? *Roger A. Freeman*—1955

States Rights and the Law of Labor Relations, *Gerard D. Reilly*—1955

Three Taft-Hartley Issues: Secondary Boycotts, "Mandatory" Injunctions, Replaced Strikers' Votes, *Theodore R. Iserman*—1955

What Price Federal Reclamation? *Raymond Moley*—1955

Private Investments Abroad, *Charles R. Carroll*—1954

Farm Price Supports—Rigid or Flexible, *Karl Brandt*—1954

*Currency Convertibility, *Gottfried Haberler*—1954

*The Control of the Location of Industry in Great Britain, *John Jewkes*—1952

*The Walsh-Healey Public Contracts Act, *John V. Van Sickle*—1952

The Economics of Full Employment: An Analysis of the U. N. Report on National and International Measures for Full Employment, *Wilhelm Röpke*—1952

Price Fixing for Foodstuffs, *Earl L. Butz*—1951

Manpower Needs and the Labor Supply, *Clarence D. Long*—1951

*An Economic Approach to Antitrust Problems, *Clare E. Griffin* — 1951

*Valley Authorities, *Raymond Moley*—1950

*Farm Price and Income Supports, *O. B. Jesness*—1950

*Monetary Policy and Economic Prosperity: Testimony of Dr. W. W. Stewart (July 3-4, 1930) before the Macmillan Committee, with introduction by *Donald B. Woodward*—1950

*Corporate Profits in Perspective, *John Linter*—1949

*Current Problems of Immigration Policy, *E. P. Hutchinson*—1949

Guaranteed Employment and Wage Plans. A Summary and Critique of the Latimer Report and Related Documents, *William A. Berridge* and *Cedric Wolfe* —1948

The Foreign Loan Policy of the United States, *J. B. Condliffe*—1947

*Proposals for Consideration by an International Conference on Trade and Employment—*J. B. Condliffe*—1946

The Market for Risk Capital, *Jules I. Bogen*—1946

Unless otherwise shown in listing, Studies 1953 and earlier, 50 cents each; 1954 to date, $1.00 each.

*Out of Print

LEGISLATIVE AND SPECIAL ANALYSES
88th Congress, Second Session, 1964

No. 1—Tax Proposals and the Federal Finances: Part V: Changes in the Proposed Revenue Act of 1964 Recommended by the Senate Committee on Finance. *Special Analysis*

No. 2—Analysis of the Fiscal 1965 Federal Budget.

No. 3—The Panama Canal—Its Past and Future.

No. 4—The Federal Government in Behavioral Science: Fields, Methods, and Funds. *Special Analysis*

No. 5—The Economic Opportunity Bill. Bills by *Sen. McNamara; Rep. Landrum*

No. 6—Urban Mass Transportation Aid Bills. Bills by *Sen. Williams; Rep. Rains*

No. 7—The Revised "War on Poverty" Bill. Bill by *Rep. Landrum*

No. 8—Social Security Amendments of 1964. Bill by *Rep. Mills*

No. 9—Presidential Disability and Vice-Presidential Vacancies.

No. 10—The Housing Act of 1964. Bill by *Sen. Sparkman*

No. 11—Proposals Relating to Reapportionment of State Legislatures and The U.S. House of Representatives.

No. 12—The Drug Safety Program. *Special Analysis*

89th Congress, First Session, 1965

No. 1—The Appalachian Regional Development Bill. Bills by *Sen. Randolph; Rep. Fallon*

No. 2—The Gold Cover Bill. Bills by *Sen. Robertson; Rep. Pat Patman*

No. 3—Legislative History and Index of AEI Publications

No. 4—Proposals to Provide Federal Aid to Elementary and Secondary Schools. Bills by *Sen. Morse; Rep. Perkins*

No. 5—Social Security Amendments of 1965. Bill by *Rep. Mills*

No. 6—Analysis of the Fiscal 1966 Federal Budget.

05